Heaven's Hidden Revolution

Terry Kashian

STUDIO
OF BOOKS
THE SPACE FOR YOUR MESSAGE

STUDIO
OF BOOKS
THE SPACE FOR YOUR MESSAGE

Studio of Books LLC
5900 Balcones Drive Suite 100
Austin, Texas 78731
www.studioofbooks.org
Hotline: (254) 800-1183

Ordering Information:
Special discounts are available on quantity purchases by corporations, associations, and others. For details, contact the publisher at the address above.

Printed in the United States of America.

ISBN-13: Softcover   978-1-964928-50-0
         Ebook   978-1-964928-51-7

Library of Congress Control Number: to follow

Contents

The Hiddenness Principle: Why Heaven's
Greatest Work Happens Underground

The Ordinary Vessel Strategy: Why
Heaven Chooses Unlikely People

Acknowledgments

To the King of kings, Jesus Christ, whose mercy, love, and power have utterly transformed my life — all honor, glory, and praise belong to You alone. This book is a testimony of Your Kingdom breaking into the lives of men and women with power and truth.

I joyfully acknowledge all those who have walked before me, beside me, and behind me, demonstrating the Spirit and power of the Kingdom of God through fearless obedience, unshakable faith, and deep compassion. Your lives have been a reflection of Heaven's heartbeat. Through your prayers, encouragement, and boldness, I have witnessed the supernatural become reality.

To those who interceded when darkness circled, who laid hands when healing was needed, who spoke life when hope dimmed — your faith stirred mine. Thank you for carrying the flame.

I give thanks for every healing I have personally received — moments when the impossible bowed to the name of Jesus. I remember the miracles, both visible and invisible, that reminded me of a God who is nearer than breath and more powerful than death.

And to the many souls who encountered the love of God through repentance and surrendered their lives to Christ — you are the true jewels in His crown. Witnessing hearts turn to Jesus has been the greatest honor of my life.

May this work serve as a tribute to the Living God whose Kingdom is advancing, whose Spirit is moving, and whose love is awakening the world.

Prologue

When the skies stir with secrets, pay attention—Heaven does not shift without reason.

Long before time measured itself in the rhythm of men's calendars, before empires cracked under the weight of their own ambitions, a truth was hidden away, veiled in light too brilliant for mortal eyes to bear. Behind the veil of the unseen, where fallen men whisper not in harmony but in rebellion, Heaven held a secret—a revolution, quiet as a breath but powerful enough to reshape existence itself.

This is not the story you were told in sacred halls or shadowed cradles. This is a tale pried from the vaults of celestial silence. A tale of seraphim who questioned, of mortals who dared, of a war not born of fire and steel, but of love disrupted and truth denied.

What if Heaven was never what we imagined? What if within its unblemished halls, a question echoed, too bold for even the stars to answer? What if rebellion was not damnation, but destiny?

You are about to step into the fracture—a place where loyalty is tested not by swords but by sacrifice, where the most radiant beings carry the heaviest doubts, and where glory does not lie in triumph but in truth.

The gates are opening. The echoes await. Let your Spirit be unshackled.

Welcome to the beginning of Heaven's Hidden Revolution.

Preface

Imagine a world where the extraordinary hides within the ordinary, where miracles unfold in the most unexpected places, and where you, yes you, are the hero of a silent initiative. This book is your invitation to step into that world.

In these pages, you'll uncover the secrets of a hidden initiative that is quietly transforming lives and communities. It's not about grand gestures or loud proclamations; it's about the subtle, powerful ways that heaven's culture is breaking into our everyday reality. This is an initiative of hope, healing, and freedom, and it starts with you.

You'll discover how ordinary people, just like you, are the chosen vessels for this divine mission. You'll learn to see the divine fingerprints in the mundane and recognize the extraordinary potential within yourself. This book will guide you through the principles and tactics that heaven uses to infiltrate and transform our world, showing you how to become an active participant in this supernatural resistance initiative.

As you read, you'll find yourself drawn into a narrative that is both deeply personal and universally significant. You'll see how small acts of kindness, moments of insight, and simple choices can ripple out to create profound change. This is not just a book; it's a call to action, a roadmap to becoming a carrier of heaven's culture in your own life.

So, turn the page and join the front lines of this hidden initiative. Your journey begins now, and the world will never be the same.

Terry Kashian

Introduction

Heaven's Hidden Revolution

Right now, as you read these words, a quiet revolution is happening all around you. It moves silently through neighborhoods, workplaces, and communities. This revolution doesn't make headlines. It doesn't announce itself with loud parades or flashy advertisements. Instead, it spreads person by person, moment by moment, like a gentle but unstoppable tide washing over our broken world. This revolution is nothing less than heaven's culture breaking into our earthly reality, bringing healing where there has been hurt, hope where there has been despair, and freedom where there has been bondage.

Heaven's culture isn't what most people think. It's not clouds and harps and boring church services that never end. It's not a set of strict religious rules or traditions that squeeze the life out of you. Heaven's culture is wildly alive, deeply practical, and more real than the chair you're sitting on right now. It's what happens when the perfect ways of God's kingdom start showing up in our imperfect world. And make no mistake—this invasion is happening whether people notice it or not.

For too long, systems of misery, depression, and poverty have dominated our world. These systems aren't just economic or political—they're spiritual at their core. They trap people in cycles of pain, convince them that nothing will ever change, and steal the hope right out of their hearts. But these systems, no matter how powerful they seem, are no match for the culture of heaven when it begins to take root.

Think about it. When was the last time you witnessed something happen that defied all logical explanation? A sudden healing that doctors couldn't explain. A relationship restored after years of bitter conflict. A community transformed from violence to peace. A person set free from addiction after countless failed attempts. These aren't just nice stories or lucky coincidences. They're evidence of heaven's culture breaking through.

The most amazing part? This divine invasion doesn't primarily use famous preachers, wealthy philanthropists, or powerful politicians as its main agents. Instead, it works through ordinary people—people just like you—who become extraordinary when they tune in to what heaven is doing. The cashier at your local grocery store might be a secret agent in this revolution. The quiet neighbor who always checks on the elderly couple down the street. The teacher who goes the extra mile for struggling students. The business owner who treats employees like family instead of resources to be used up. These everyday heroes often have no idea they're part of something so much bigger than themselves.

By picking up this book, you've just stepped onto the front lines of this hidden revolution. You've made a decision—whether you fully realize it yet or not—to open your eyes to what's been happening all around you. And more than that, you've taken the first step toward becoming an active participant in this supernatural resistance movement that is silently but surely dismantling systems of darkness and building something beautiful in their place.

This revolution will transform not just your understanding of spiritual reality but your actual neighborhood. The changes begin in the unseen realm but quickly become visible to anyone paying attention. A supernatural ripple effect starts with one person, then spreads to families, workplaces, schools, and entire communities. Nothing stays the same when heaven's culture takes root.

Beyond Religious Performance

Let me be clear about something right from the start. What we're talking about has nothing to do with religious performance. It has nothing to do with saying the right prayers, attending the right services, wearing the right clothes, or using the right spiritual-sounding words. Those things might look good on the outside, but they often lack the life-changing power that comes from authentic connection with divine reality.

Too many people have been hurt by empty religion. They've seen the gap between what gets preached on Sunday and what happens on Monday. They've felt the sting of judgment from those who claim to represent God but show little of His love. They've grown tired of spiritual talk that never translates into real transformation. If that's been your experience, I want you to know that this book isn't offering more of the same. We're going in a completely different direction.

What sets this divine invasion apart is that it bypasses human limitations altogether. It doesn't depend on perfect people or perfect circumstances. It doesn't require religious credentials or special titles. It works despite our weaknesses and sometimes even through them. This invasion operates according to heaven's rules, not earth's, which means it often shows up in ways that religious experts completely miss.

In the pages that follow, you'll discover five supernatural "invasion tactics" that heaven uses to transform earth. These tactics aren't complicated spiritual formulas that only work for super-spiritual people. They're simple, practical approaches that anyone can learn. They're the same patterns that have been changing lives and communities throughout history, often without anyone recognizing the divine strategy behind them.

You'll also learn how to tell the difference between mere human goodness and truly divine breakthroughs. This distinction is crucial because not everything that looks spiritual actually comes from heaven. Some efforts, though well-intentioned, are just people trying to fix problems in their own strength. These human solutions might bring temporary relief but rarely lead to lasting transformation. Divine breakthroughs, on the other hand, create changes that defy explanation and stand the test of time.

Perhaps most importantly, you'll experience a radical shift in how you see the ordinary moments of your day. That unexpected conversation with a stranger. The random thought that won't leave your mind. The sudden urge to reach out to someone you haven't talked to in years. The dream that feels more real than waking life. Once you understand how heaven's invasion works, you'll start to recognize these moments not as meaningless coincidences but as potential doorways for divine activity.

Unlike many spiritual books that offer theory without substance, this guide provides practical tools for participating in heaven's infiltration strategy. You won't just read about what God is doing—you'll learn how to join in. The focus isn't on giving you more information but on helping you develop spiritual discernment so you can recognize and respond to divine opportunities when they appear.

This isn't about becoming more religious. It's about becoming more tuned in to the frequency of heaven so you can play your unique part in this cosmic revolution. It's about learning to see with new eyes and hear with new ears. It's about discovering that you—yes, you—have been designed to be a carrier of heaven's culture into the specific places and relationships that make up your life.

Your Infiltration Handbook

Think of this book as your personal infiltration handbook. It contains field-tested wisdom gathered from countless ordinary people who have stumbled into extraordinary divine moments. Some knew exactly what they were doing. Others had no idea they were being used as agents of heaven's culture until they looked back and saw the trail of transformation behind them.

Over the coming chapters, we'll explore the hidden principles of kingdom infiltration. These principles aren't new—they've been operating since the beginning of time. But they often get buried under layers of religious tradition or dismissed as outdated by modern thinking. When properly understood and applied, these principles release a kind of spiritual power that no human system can ultimately resist.

We'll look at real stories of ordinary people who became extraordinary agents of divine change. People from all walks of life, all backgrounds, all personality types. The shy accountant who somehow found himself leading a movement of generosity that rescued a dying town. The former drug addict whose simple acts of kindness sparked healing in a violence-plagued neighborhood. The overworked single mom whose persistent prayers opened doors that professionals had declared permanently closed. These stories will show you what's possible when heaven's culture finds willing partners on earth.

The core lesson running through everything we'll explore is simple but profound: heaven's transformation doesn't require religious credentials, just ordinary people willing to follow divine promptings. This truth has revolutionary implications. It means that no one is disqualified from participating in this divine invasion. Your past mistakes don't disqualify you. Your lack of biblical knowledge doesn't disqualify you. Your doubts and questions don't disqualify you. In fact, heaven often works most powerfully through the people who feel least qualified.

We'll also examine the critical difference between cultural Christianity and the authentic culture of heaven. They might look similar on the surface, but they operate according to completely different principles. Cultural Christianity focuses on maintaining appearances and traditions. Heaven's culture focuses on bringing genuine transformation. Cultural Christianity draws lines between insiders and outsiders. Heaven's culture constantly pushes boundaries to include the excluded. Cultural Christianity settles for managing sin. Heaven's culture uproots it entirely and plants something beautiful in its place.

Throughout this handbook, you'll find practical exercises designed to sharpen your spiritual senses. These aren't complicated rituals or mystical practices. They're simple ways to become more aware of what heaven is already doing around you. The more you practice these exercises, the more naturally you'll start to recognize divine opportunities in everyday situations. What once seemed like random events will begin to form patterns. What once felt like meaningless coincidences will reveal themselves as divine appointments.

You'll also discover how to overcome the common obstacles that prevent people from fully participating in heaven's invasion. Fear of looking foolish. Doubt about whether God would really use someone like you. Confusion about what's really from God and what's just your own thoughts. Past disappointments that make you hesitant to hope again. We'll address these obstacles head-on with practical wisdom and encouragement drawn from those who have faced and overcome the same challenges.

The invasion of heaven's culture isn't happening because earth deserves it. It's happening because love can't help but give itself away. The same love that spoke the universe into existence is speaking new realities into your neighborhood right now. The same power that raised Jesus from the dead is working to raise dead situations and relationships all around you. And you've been invited to be part of this divine conspiracy of kindness that is slowly but surely changing everything.

So turn the page. Step further into the adventure. Learn to see what most people miss and to participate in what heaven is already doing. The revolution is happening with or without you. But it becomes so much richer, so much more wonderful, when you play your part.

The Hiddenness Principle: Why Heaven's Greatest Work Happens Underground

The Counterintuitive Strategy

The most powerful things in the world often grow in the dark. Seeds crack open underground, far from human eyes. Babies develop in the hidden space of the womb. The strongest roots of mighty trees spread beneath the soil where no one sees them. This pattern shows up again and again in nature. The most important growth happens out of sight before anything becomes visible above the surface.

Heaven works the same way.

The biggest spiritual breakthroughs rarely start with loud announcements or public displays. They begin quietly, secretly, often in the most overlooked places with the most overlooked people. This is not an accident. It is a deliberate strategy.

Think about how water shapes rock. It doesn't attack with dramatic force all at once. Instead, it seeps into tiny cracks. It freezes and expands. It flows around obstacles. Day after day, year after year, the gentle but persistent action of water transforms even the hardest stone. Heaven's work follows this same pattern, gradually reshaping the hardest human systems and situations not through dramatic confrontation but through gentle, persistent influence that most people never notice until the transformation is already well underway.

This approach makes no sense to human thinking. We expect important things to come with fanfare. We want spotlights and stage announcements and impressive credentials. We believe real change requires big budgets, famous names, and massive organizations. The idea that world-changing power might be flowing through ordinary moments and ordinary people seems ridiculous. But this is exactly how heaven prefers to work.

The hiddenness principle turns our expectations upside down. It reveals that heaven's most significant movements often start small, develop underground, and spread through networks invisible to those not paying attention. These movements rarely have official names or headquarters. They don't send fundraising letters or hold press conferences. They simply spread from person to person, heart to heart, situation to situation, bringing life and transformation wherever they go.

Look at history's most powerful spiritual awakenings. Almost without exception, they began not with religious leaders but with ordinary people meeting in homes, workplaces, and unexpected locations. The official religious institutions typically noticed these movements only after they were already changing the cultural landscape. By then, it was too late to stop them. The underground river had already carved new channels through the hardened ground of society.

This pattern appears repeatedly in ancient spiritual texts. The divine doesn't choose the obvious candidates for important missions. Instead, it picks the youngest son, the foreign woman, the shepherd boy, the tax collector, the fisherman. Time after time, heaven bypasses the religious experts and works through people with no credentials or influence. This isn't just an interesting historical footnote. It's a revelation of how heaven still operates today.

Hidden in Plain Sight

The most effective disguise isn't an elaborate costume. It's ordinary clothes that blend perfectly with the surroundings. Heaven's work often wears exactly this kind of disguise. It doesn't announce itself with supernatural special effects. It slips into everyday reality through events most people dismiss as coincidence, chance, or random good fortune.

That unexpected phone call from an old friend who mentions exactly what you needed to hear. The book that falls off the shelf in front of you, opening to a page with the precise wisdom you've been searching for. The stranger who says something in passing that answers a question you've been wrestling with for months. The job loss that feels like disaster but leads to the opportunity you would never have found otherwise. These moments aren't accidents. They're divine activity hidden in plain sight.

Most people experience these "coincidences" regularly but never connect the dots. They miss the pattern forming right before their eyes. They fail to recognize the deliberate intelligence orchestrating these seemingly random events. But once you understand the hiddenness principle, you start to see evidence of heaven's fingerprints everywhere.

Consider how many life-changing conversations happen in the most ordinary places. Coffee shops. Grocery store aisles. School pickup lines. Bus stops. These unremarkable locations become holy ground when heaven slips into human interaction. The divine doesn't need stained glass and organ music to show up. It prefers the ordinary spaces where people live their daily lives.

Even the timing of these divine encounters often comes disguised. The flat tire that makes you late for work—and prevents you from being involved in the accident ahead. The missed flight that seems like terrible luck—until you meet the person next to you during the delay who changes the course of your life. The illness that keeps you home—just in time to receive the call you would have missed otherwise. Heaven's timing rarely makes sense at the moment. Its perfect orchestration usually becomes clear only in retrospect.

This disguised activity isn't meant to be confusing. It serves an important purpose. It requires us to develop spiritual perception that goes beyond surface appearances. It trains us to look deeper, to question our automatic assumptions, to recognize patterns that most people miss. In short, it teaches us to see reality as it actually is, not just as it appears to be.

The ability to spot heaven's disguised activity is like developing a new sense. At first, you catch only glimpses. You notice connections between events that seemed unrelated. You sense meaning in moments that would have previously seemed random. But with practice, this perception grows stronger. You begin to anticipate divine movements before they fully emerge. You learn to position yourself at the intersection of heaven and earth, ready to participate in breakthroughs that others never see coming.

The Underground Network

Right now in your city, an invisible network is operating. It has no official name. No headquarters. No organizational chart. Yet it functions with remarkable effectiveness, systematically addressing problems that have resisted official solutions for years.

This network consists of ordinary people who have stumbled into extraordinary assignments. The retired teacher who starts mentoring neighborhood kids and unknowingly interrupts generational cycles of poverty. The business owner who treats employees with unusual dignity and creates a pocket of heaven's culture in the marketplace. The artist whose work bypasses intellectual barriers and speaks directly to hearts that have been closed to spiritual reality. The parent whose consistent love provides a living picture of divine care to everyone who enters their home.

These people rarely see themselves as spiritual giants. Most would laugh if you called them heroes. They're simply doing what they feel compelled to do, following inner promptings they can't fully explain. Yet together, their seemingly disconnected actions form a coherent strategy that gradually dismantles strongholds of darkness and establishes outposts of heaven's culture throughout the city.

What makes this network so powerful is precisely its underground nature. It doesn't depend on official permission or recognition. It can't be controlled by religious or political authorities. It spreads through relationships rather than organization, influence rather than force. Like an underground root system, it can survive even when visible structures are removed. Cut it in one place, and it simply grows in another.

The members of this network often don't know each other. The homeless shelter volunteer has no idea that her work connects with the high school teacher across town who mentors at-risk students, or with the former addict who now counsels people struggling with substance abuse. Yet heaven sees these separate efforts as part of a unified campaign. Each person addresses a different aspect of the same larger issues, creating a comprehensive response that no single organization could coordinate.

This invisible web extends through every sector of society. It includes people of different backgrounds, ages, education levels, and social classes. Some have formal religious affiliations. Others abandoned organized religion years ago. Some would use spiritual language to describe what they're doing. Others would simply say they're trying to make their corner of the world a little better. But heaven recognizes them all as part of the same underground movement.

The power of this network comes not from its individual members but from the divine intelligence connecting their efforts. Like cells in a body, each person performs a specific function while contributing to the health of the whole system. No one needs to understand the entire strategy to play their part effectively. They simply need to respond faithfully to the assignments that come their way, trusting that their piece fits into a larger picture they may never fully see.

What would happen if these underground agents became aware of each other? What if they began to recognize themselves as part of the same divine conspiracy? Not to create a new organization or institution, but simply to encourage each other and perhaps collaborate when their assignments overlap? The resulting synergy would multiply their impact many times over.

Why Hiddenness Protects the Mission

Hiddenness isn't just a divine preference. It's a strategic necessity. It protects heaven's work during its most vulnerable early stages, allowing deep roots to develop before facing opposition.

Think about how resistance works. Systems of darkness can't fight what they can't see or understand. They're designed to identify and neutralize obvious threats. They have well-established responses to direct challenges. But they have no effective defense against transformation that comes through unexpected channels. By the time they recognize what's happening, the new reality has already taken root too deeply to be easily removed.

History shows this pattern clearly. The most effective movements for spiritual and social transformation didn't announce their intentions with dramatic manifestos. They spread quietly through small gatherings in homes and seemingly insignificant acts of courage and compassion. By the time authorities recognized the threat to their control, these movements had already created alternative communities too resilient to be stamped out by persecution.

The same principle applies today. When heaven's culture enters a workplace, neighborhood, or family system, it rarely arrives with dramatic confrontation. Instead, it begins with small acts of integrity, kindness, and truth-telling that seem harmless to existing power structures. These acts create tiny cracks in the prevailing culture. Over time, those cracks widen. New possibilities emerge. Alternative ways of relating become visible. Before long, the old system finds itself facing a fully formed alternative that emerged right under its nose.

Premature exposure often triggers unnecessary opposition. When divine initiatives draw too much attention too quickly, they face resistance before they're strong enough to withstand it. Religious institutions try to control them. Political powers try to co-opt them. Media attention distorts their essence. The original simplicity and power get lost in controversy, personality conflicts, and organizational politics.

Even well-meaning publicity can damage genuine spiritual advancements. When people try to package and promote what heaven is doing, they often freeze a fluid movement into rigid programs. They reduce living principles to formulas. They turn authentic experience into performance. What began as fresh wind from heaven became another stale religious product.

This explains why many of heaven's most effective agents maintain a low profile. It's not false humility or unnecessary secrecy. It's wisdom.

They understand that drawing attention to themselves would actually hinder the work they've been given to do. They're content to remain relatively unknown as long as transformation continues to spread through their influence.

The hiddenness principle also explains why divine activity often pauses or redirects when people try to commercialize or institutionalize it. Heaven resists human attempts to control, systematize, or profit from genuine spiritual advancements. The moment someone tries to build an empire around what was meant to remain fluid and freely given, the divine life begins to drain away. What remains may look impressive from the outside, but it no longer carries the same transformative power.

This doesn't mean all public ministry or organized efforts are wrong. There are seasons when heaven's work emerges into full visibility, ready to withstand the scrutiny and opposition it will inevitably attract. The key is timing. Premature exposure damages the mission. But hiding something that's ready to be revealed limits its impact. Discerning the difference requires spiritual sensitivity and wisdom.

Recap: Embracing Divine Hiddenness

The hiddenness principle changes everything about how we recognize and participate in heaven's work on earth. It shifts our attention from the spectacular to the subtle, from the center stage to the margins, from the famous to the overlooked. It teaches us to value what remains unseen as much as what appears on the surface.

You now understand that heaven's most powerful work deliberately happens beneath the surface. This isn't a bug in the system—it's a feature. The divine strategy intentionally bypasses human expectations about how spiritual gains should look. It targets the foundations rather than the facades, knowing that lasting transformation must begin at the root level of culture and consciousness.

You've learned how heaven's activity disguises itself in everyday events. Those "coincidences" that keep showing up in your life form a deliberate pattern. They represent divine intelligence at work, creating opportunities that most people miss but that can lead to extraordinary gains when recognized and embraced. These disguised divine moments surround you every day, hiding in plain sight amid the ordinary details of your life.

You've discovered the reality of an invisible network operating in your city. This underground web of heaven's agents includes people who may never enter a church building or use religious language. Yet their seemingly random acts of obedience form part of a coherent strategy to establish outposts of divine culture throughout your community. Some of these agents might be people you interact with regularly without recognizing their spiritual significance.

You now grasp why hiddenness protects heaven's mission during its vulnerable early stages. Premature exposure often triggers resistance that can damage genuine spiritual movements before they're strong enough to withstand opposition. This explains why many authentic breakthroughs develop quietly for extended periods before becoming publicly visible. It also reveals the wisdom of maintaining a low profile while carrying out divine assignments.

So what does this mean for your daily life? Start noticing the disguised divine activity all around you. Those "random" thoughts that keep returning to your mind. The unexpected connections between seemingly unrelated events. The doors that open and close in patterns too precise to be coincidence. Train yourself to see what others miss.

Begin journaling the unexpected coincidences that might be heaven's fingerprints in your life. Write down those moments when exactly what you needed arrived at exactly the right time. Record the unusual thoughts or promptings that led to meaningful encounters. Look for patterns in these experiences. Over time, you'll develop a personal record of divine activity that will strengthen your ability to recognize heaven's movements.

Connect with others who sense the hidden movement happening around them. Not to create a new organization or program, but simply to compare notes and encourage each other. These conversations often reveal connections between what seemed like isolated experiences. They help confirm that you're not imagining things—you're actually perceiving a reality that others miss.

Most importantly, resist the urge to publicize or institutionalize genuine divine gains too quickly. Learn to value hiddenness as a protective covering rather than an obstacle to overcome. Be content to remain in the background if that's where your assignment is most effective. Understand that fame and public recognition often hinder rather than help heaven's deepest work.

The hiddenness principle doesn't diminish the significance of what you're doing. It actually elevates it. In heaven's economy, the most important work often happens where human eyes never see it. The person faithfully loving difficult family members may be accomplishing more than the celebrity preaching to thousands. The quiet acts of integrity in a corrupt workplace might be more strategic than dramatic public confrontations. The prayers offered in a private room may change more than the declarations made from public platforms.

As you embrace this principle, you'll find freedom from the need for human recognition and validation. You'll discover the joy of participating in divine activity for its own sake, not for the approval it might bring. You'll learn to value results over recognition, transformation over attention, and lasting fruit over temporary fame.

The greatest heroes in heaven's narrative are often people whose names history never recorded. Their impact continues generations after their deaths, though few connect current blessings to their hidden faithfulness. They understood what many miss—that obscurity is not a hindrance to significance but often the very condition that makes the deepest impact possible.

You may be one of those hidden heroes right now, faithfully carrying out assignments that few notice or appreciate. If so, take heart. Heaven sees what others miss. Your seemingly small acts of obedience form part of a divine strategy more sophisticated and far-reaching than you can imagine. Though the full results may remain invisible during your lifetime, you are helping to establish outposts of heaven's culture that will continue to transform reality long after you're gone.

The Ordinary Vessel Strategy: Why Heaven Chooses Unlikely People

The Qualification Paradox

Heaven plays by different rules than earth. This simple truth explains so much about how divine power shows up in our world. While human systems value impressive credentials, extensive training, and social influence, heaven consistently chooses to work through the most unlikely people. This isn't a mistake or a temporary approach. It's a deliberate strategy that has been used throughout history.

Think about who gets picked for important jobs in our world. Companies want candidates with the right degrees from the best schools. They look for impressive resumes with years of relevant experience. They seek out people with proven track records and stellar recommendations. This makes perfect sense from a human perspective. Why wouldn't you want the most qualified person for an important position?

But heaven turns this entire system upside down. Time after time, the divine passes over the religious experts, the wealthy donors, the influential leaders, and the people with perfect spiritual resumes. Instead, heaven deliberately selects the overlooked, the untrained, the socially awkward, and even the seriously flawed to carry out its most important missions.

This creates what we might call the qualification paradox: the very things that qualify you in human systems often disqualify you in heaven's system, while the very things that disqualify you in human systems often qualify you in heaven's. This paradox isn't just interesting—it's revolutionary in its implications for who can participate in spiritual breakthroughs.

History reveals this pattern with remarkable consistency. The ancient texts show divine power flowing through shepherds rather than scholars, tax collectors rather than religious teachers, and fishermen rather than the politically connected. The pattern continues throughout history, with spiritual awakenings repeatedly starting among the poor and marginalized rather than the religious elite.

But why? Why would heaven consistently bypass the seemingly qualified in favor of the obviously unqualified? The answer reveals something profound about how divine power operates in our world.

First, ordinary vessels create undeniable results. When someone with impressive credentials achieves something great, people naturally attribute the success to that person's talent, education, or experience. But when someone with obvious limitations achieves the same results, people have to look elsewhere for an explanation. The gap between the vessel's limitations and the extraordinary results points directly to a power source beyond human ability.

Second, ordinary vessels stay dependent on divine power rather than their own abilities. Those with impressive qualifications naturally tend to rely on their training, experience, and proven methods. They trust what has worked for them in the past. Ordinary vessels have no such luxury. Their limitations force them to depend on divine guidance and power for every step. This ongoing dependence creates a continuous flow of supernatural resources that self-reliant people rarely access.

Third, ordinary vessels remain flexible and teachable. Religious experts often become locked into rigid thinking patterns and established methods. They have professional reputations to protect and theological positions to defend. Ordinary people typically have fewer preconceptions about how divine power "should" work and fewer religious frameworks limiting what they're willing to try. This openness makes them more responsive to fresh divine guidance.

The qualification paradox explains why spiritual breakthroughs often start at the margins of society rather than the center, among the overlooked rather than the obvious leaders. It's not that heaven has anything against education, training, or experience. It's that these human qualifications often come with hidden liabilities that make it harder for divine power to flow freely.

Your Disqualifications as Divine Qualifications

Most people carry a mental list of reasons why heaven couldn't possibly use them for anything important. Maybe you have such a list yourself. Your past mistakes. Your lack of biblical knowledge. Your limited education. Your social awkwardness. Your ongoing struggles with certain habits or attitudes. Your lack of leadership experience. Your financial problems. Your health challenges. The list goes on and on.

What if you've been reading the list upside down? What if these very things you see as disqualifications are actually what qualify you to be a perfect vessel for divine purposes?

This sounds crazy from a human perspective. We've been trained to hide our weaknesses, compensate for our limitations, and present the most impressive version of ourselves possible. The idea that our flaws might actually be spiritual assets seems completely backward. Yet this is precisely how heaven's strategy works.

Your failures and mistakes create a capacity for compassion that success never could. The person who has failed deeply knows what it's like to need grace. They can extend genuine mercy to others without the condescension that often accompanies help from those who have never seriously stumbled. Your past failures, rather than disqualifying you, may have been preparing you to reach people that "perfect" religious representatives never could.

Your lack of religious knowledge might protect you from the complications that often come with too much theological training. While understanding spiritual principles is valuable, too much emphasis on abstract knowledge can actually interfere with simple obedience. Many religious scholars become so focused on analyzing divine truth that they struggle to actually apply it. Your simpler understanding might allow you to respond more directly to divine guidance without overthinking everything.

Your social awkwardness or lack of charisma might be your greatest asset in a world drowning in slick presentations and manipulative personalities. People are increasingly suspicious of polished communicators and natural charmers. They hunger for authenticity even when it comes in imperfect packages. Your obvious humanness might create trust that smooth professionalism never could.

Even your ongoing struggles can become divine qualifications. The areas where you continually need grace become the very places you can offer genuine hope to others facing similar challenges. Your weakness creates space for divine strength to become visible. Your struggles keep you humble and dependent rather than self sufficient and proud.

Consider how this plays out in real situations. The business leader with a perfect track record may have difficulty relating to employees who are struggling. But the leader who has experienced failure and recovery brings wisdom and compassion that perfection never produces. The parent who has made serious mistakes and found healing can guide other parents through similar challenges with genuine understanding rather than judgment.

Your specific limitations create unique opportunities for divine power to become visible. When you succeed despite obvious gaps in your qualifications, people naturally look beyond you for explanations. They recognize that something more than human ability must be at work. This draws attention to the divine source rather than the human vessel—which is precisely the point.

The areas where you feel most disqualified may be exactly where heaven wants to work most powerfully through you. Not by magically removing your limitations, but by manifesting divine power through those very limitations. Like light shining through cracks in a clay pot, divine brilliance becomes most visible where the vessel is most obviously flawed.

This doesn't mean you should never grow or develop your abilities. Personal growth is valuable. But it does mean you don't need to wait until you've overcome all your limitations before heaven can use you. In fact, trying to perfect yourself first might actually interfere with the divine strategy that deliberately works through imperfect vessels.

The Power of Unimpressive People

Something remarkable happens when heaven works through ordinary, unimpressive people. The results bypass human ego and religious performance. They create a kind of evidence that even skeptics find difficult to dismiss.

When spiritual results come through famous religious figures with powerful platforms, people naturally question whether personality, psychology, or social dynamics might explain what happened. But when the same results come through the shy accountant next door or the formerly addicted construction worker down the street, those explanations fall short. The gap between the vessel and the results becomes too wide to explain away.

This creates what we might call "undeniable evidence"—not in the sense that no one can deny it (people can deny almost anything), but in the sense that the most reasonable explanation points to something beyond human ability. When obviously limited people produce extraordinary transformation, even hardened skeptics sometimes pause to reconsider their assumptions about reality.

History shows this pattern repeatedly. spiritual awakenings rarely start with religious professionals. They typically begin with ordinary people who stumble into extraordinary experiences of divine reality. The professional ministers usually join later, after the evidence becomes too compelling to ignore. By then, the movement has already established its authenticity through results that can't be explained by human factors alone.

The power of unimpressive people explains why some of the most effective spiritual healers have no formal training or credentials. Their results speak for themselves. It explains why some of the most transformative community initiatives start with unlikely leaders who simply responded to a need they couldn't ignore. It explains why some of the most life-changing spiritual conversations happen with people who would never be hired as professional ministers.

Heaven's preference for ordinary vessels creates a kind of spiritual meritocracy where results matter more than appearances. It doesn't matter what degrees hang on your wall, what title precedes your name, or how impressively you perform religious rituals. What matters is whether lives are genuinely transformed through your influence. This standard cuts through religious politics, institutional barriers, and human prejudices to create space for authentic spiritual power to flow wherever it finds willing vessels.

The ordinary vessel strategy also creates unique protection against pride and self-importance. When heaven works through obviously limited people, they typically remain acutely aware that the power comes through them, not from them. They can't easily fool themselves into thinking their own abilities produced the results they're seeing. This awareness keeps the channel open for continued divine flow that might otherwise be blocked by ego and self-reliance.

Throughout history, spiritual gains have repeatedly come through the most unexpected people. The uneducated visionary whose simple message transforms a community. The recovering addict whose newfound compassion reaches people that religious professionals never could. The socially awkward teenager whose authentic faith inspires an entire generation of friends. These unlikely vessels don't succeed despite their limitations but often because of them.

When divine power flows through ordinary people, it creates a contagious hope that anyone can participate in spiritual breakthroughs. If heaven can work through that person with all their obvious flaws and limitations, maybe it can work through me too. This hope mobilizes far more people than any system that elevates special individuals with rare qualifications. It democratizes spiritual power, making it available to anyone willing to respond to divine promptings regardless of their human credentials.

Breaking the Religious Expert Paradigm

Our culture trains us to depend on experts. We expect doctors to heal our bodies, therapists to heal our emotions, and religious professionals to heal our souls. This expert-dependent system creates passive consumers who wait for specialists to solve their problems rather than participating actively in the solutions.

Heaven systematically undermines this dependence by consistently producing greater spiritual results through ordinary people than through religious experts. This isn't because expertise has no value. It's because over-reliance on human expertise often interferes with direct divine activity.

The religious expert paradigm creates several problems that heaven's ordinary vessel strategy directly addresses.

First, it concentrates spiritual power in the hands of a small professional class rather than distributing it throughout the community. When people believe only special individuals with extensive training can access and channel divine power, they naturally become passive recipients rather than active participants. They watch from the sidelines while the "qualified" people do the important spiritual work. Heaven breaks this pattern by demonstrating that ordinary people with no special training can experience and transmit divine reality just as effectively—sometimes more effectively—than religious professionals.

Second, the expert paradigm creates unhealthy dependency relationships that ultimately limit spiritual growth. People become attached to human intermediaries rather than developing their own direct connection with divine reality. They rely on the pastor's prayers rather than learning to pray effectively themselves. They depend on the teacher's insights rather than developing their own spiritual discernment. Heaven disrupts this dependency by regularly bypassing the expected channels and flowing directly through unlikely individuals.

Third, religious professionalism often leads to performance-based spirituality where appearance matters more than authenticity. Ministers feel pressure to maintain a certain image regardless of their actual spiritual condition. Congregants learn to perform the expected religious behaviors rather than pursuing genuine transformation. The ordinary vessel strategy breaks this performance trap by demonstrating that heaven values honest weakness over religious pretense.

Throughout history, divine activity has consistently flowed outside official religious channels whenever those channels became too rigid, politicized, or disconnected from genuine spiritual power. This pattern isn't anti-leadership or antiorganization. It's simply heaven's way of preserving authentic spiritual connection when human systems begin to interfere with rather than facilitate divine flow.

The ordinary vessel strategy reminds us that spiritual reality can't be contained within professional structures or controlled by institutional authorities. It flows wherever it finds openness, regardless of human credentials or official position. This doesn't mean organizations and leadership have no value. It simply means they function best when they recognize and support heaven's work through ordinary people rather than trying to monopolize or control that work.

When heaven consistently produces greater fruit through ordinary people than through religious professionals, it creates a healthy recalibration of the entire spiritual ecosystem. Professional ministers who recognize this pattern stop seeing themselves as the primary channels of divine activity and start seeing themselves as equippers and supporters of what heaven is doing through everyone. Ordinary people stop waiting for the professionals to solve spiritual problems and start responding directly to divine guidance. The whole community becomes more responsive to heaven's activity rather than dependent on human intermediaries.

This shift from expert-dependency to direct divine partnership represents one of the most significant spiritual developments happening in our time. All across the world, ordinary people are discovering they can experience and transmit divine reality without waiting for permission or mediation from religious authorities. This doesn't diminish the value of wise spiritual leadership. It simply places that leadership in its proper context as supportive rather than controlling.

Recap: Embracing Your Ordinary Vessel Status

You've now discovered the revolutionary ordinary vessel strategy that heaven uses to transform earth. This isn't just interesting information—it's an invitation to see yourself and your role in divine purposes in a completely new light.

You've learned how heaven deliberately chooses unlikely people, bypassing those with impressive credentials in favor of those whose limitations actually make them more effective channels for divine power. This qualification paradox turns our normal understanding of spiritual qualification upside down, revealing that heaven values different qualities than human systems do.

You've discovered that your perceived disqualifications—your failures, weaknesses, lack of religious knowledge, or social awkwardness—are precisely what heaven values as perfect entry points for divine partnership. The very aspects of your life that you thought made you unusable may actually be your greatest spiritual assets.

You've seen how unimpressive people produce undeniable results when divine power flows through their limitations. The gap between the obvious inadequacy of the vessel and the extraordinary nature of the results creates a kind of evidence that points directly to supernatural activity rather than human ability.

You've understood how heaven's ordinary vessel strategy systematically undermines our unhealthy dependence on spiritual celebrities, professional ministers, and religious authorities by consistently producing greater fruit through ordinary people who simply follow divine promptings.

So what does this mean for your daily life? Start by identifying the aspects of yourself that you've considered spiritual disqualifications. Your past mistakes. Your ongoing struggles. Your lack of religious training. Your personality quirks. Instead of seeing these as obstacles to overcome before heaven can use you, recognize them as potential divine qualifications that create space for supernatural power to become visible.

Begin paying attention to divine invitations that come outside religious channels. That random thought that won't leave your mind. The unexpected opportunity that doesn't fit your spiritual resume. The person you feel drawn to help despite having no special qualifications to address their needs. These seemingly random promptings often represent heaven's ordinary vessel strategy at work in your life.

Celebrate the freedom that comes from not needing to impress others with your spirituality. You don't have to pretend to be more knowledgeable, more consistent, or more put-together than you actually are. Heaven specifically chooses ordinary, flawed people so that the results will clearly come from divine power rather than human ability. Your limitations aren't obstacles to overcome—they're features that make you a perfect candidate for heaven's work.

Look for other ordinary vessels who are experiencing supernatural results in their lives. Not the famous spiritual personalities with large platforms, but the unimpressive people in your own community who somehow catalyze divine activity wherever they go. Connect with these unlikely spiritual catalysts. Learn from their experiences. Notice how heaven works through their limitations rather than despite them.

Most importantly, stop waiting until you feel qualified before responding to divine promptings. If you wait until you've overcome all your weaknesses, developed impressive spiritual knowledge, and achieved consistent victory in every area of your life, you'll never participate in heaven's work. The ordinary vessel strategy specifically selects people who know they aren't qualified in themselves and therefore remain dependent on divine guidance and power for every step.

This doesn't mean you should never grow or develop your spiritual understanding. Growth is valuable. But it does mean you don't need to wait until you've reached some imaginary threshold of qualification before heaven can work through you. In fact, remaining aware of your limitations creates precisely the kind of dependency on divine power that makes you an ideal vessel.

The ordinary vessel strategy reveals that heaven values availability over ability, responsiveness over resources, and genuine dependency over religious performance. This means that no matter who you are, where you've been, or what limitations you currently face, you qualify as a potential agent of divine breakthrough in your world.

So stop disqualifying yourself based on human standards that heaven doesn't use. Stop waiting for permission from religious authorities to respond to divine promptings. Stop comparing yourself to spiritual celebrities whose platforms may actually make them less effective vessels than you are. Start embracing your ordinary vessel status as a divine strategy rather than a human limitation.

Heaven's infiltration of earth happens primarily through people who have no impressive spiritual credentials—just an openness to divine guidance and a willingness to act on what they receive. Their impact comes not from their exceptional abilities but from the exceptional power that flows through their ordinary lives. You can be one of those people starting today, not by becoming more impressive, but by embracing the divine qualification of being obviously unqualified in yourself.

The Divine Discernment Crisis: Good vs. God

The Dangerous Counterfeit

Good things happen every day. A stranger helps an elderly woman cross the street. A teacher stays late to tutor a struggling student. A neighbor mows the lawn for a sick friend. We see these acts and feel warm inside. We call them good—and they are. But not all good things come from heaven.

Human goodness fills our world. It shows up as kind acts, positive thinking, moral behavior, and helpful programs. These things matter. They make life better. They ease suffering. They bring moments of light to dark situations. No one can argue with the value of human goodness in a world that often feels cold and uncaring.

But here's the problem that almost no one talks about: human goodness can become the most effective barrier to genuine heaven-originated transformation. It creates a dangerous counterfeit that looks so much like the real thing that most people never notice the difference. This counterfeit satisfies our desire to help others and feel spiritually connected without requiring the deeper surrender that divine activity demands.

Think about counterfeit money. The most dangerous counterfeits aren't the obvious fakes that anyone can spot. They're sophisticated copies that look almost identical to the real thing. They have the right paper, the right ink, the right security features. Only experts with special training can tell the difference. Human goodness works the same way. It mimics divine activity so closely that most people—even spiritually minded people—mistake one for the other.

When we do good things from our best human intentions, we create positive results. People get helped. Problems get solved. Communities improve. These outcomes feel satisfying. They meet real needs. They align with many spiritual values. But they remain fundamentally different from the transformation that happens when heaven directly initiates activity through responsive human partners.

The difference matters because human goodness, no matter how impressive, has built-in limitations. It can treat symptoms but rarely reaches root causes. It depends on human energy that eventually runs out. It stays within the boundaries of what seems reasonable and possible. It improves situations without fundamentally transforming them. Divine activity, by contrast, addresses root causes, draws on endless resources, regularly exceeds human limitations, and creates genuine transformation rather than mere improvement.

Most of us never learn to tell the difference. We grow up in cultures that celebrate human goodness without distinguishing it from divine activity. Our religious institutions often focus more on making us good people than on connecting us with the source of divine life. We learn to value moral behavior, positive attitudes, and helpful actions without recognizing that these things, while valuable, fall short of the supernatural transformation that heaven offers.

This confusion creates a crisis of discernment that affects even the most spiritually sincere people. We mistake human goodness for divine activity and wonder why our efforts, though well-intentioned, produce limited results. We exhaust ourselves trying to generate through human effort what can only come through divine initiative. We settle for being nice when we could be channels of supernatural transformation.

Beyond Religious Moralism

Religious performance creates an even more convincing counterfeit than ordinary human goodness. It dresses up human effort in spiritual language. It follows ancient patterns and practices. It uses the right words and observes the right rituals. It feels more spiritual than secular goodness because it includes God in the conversation.

Yet much religious activity remains just as human-originated as any secular good deed. The source is still our effort, our discipline, our determination to be good. We simply wrap it in spiritual packaging and call it divine. This religious moralism—the pursuit of being "good Christians" or "good spiritual people"—can actually become the most effective immunization against authentic divine life.

How does this happen? When we focus on becoming good religious performers, we create a substitute that satisfies our spiritual hunger just enough to prevent us from seeking the real thing. Like eating junk food when our bodies need nutrition, religious performance temporarily fills the spiritual hunger without providing the divine life we actually need. We mistake religious activity for spiritual transformation and wonder why we still feel empty inside despite doing all the right things.

The culture of heaven dismantles not just obvious evil but also this subtle counterfeit of religious performance. It exposes how our attempts to be "good Christians" often keep us from experiencing the authentic divine life that transforms from the inside out rather than conforming from the outside in. It reveals how easily we substitute human religious effort for genuine spiritual connection.

Religious systems typically reward external conformity rather than internal transformation. They create environments where looking good becomes more important than being real. They establish performance metrics that measure religious activities rather than genuine spiritual fruit. They produce people who know how to act spiritual without necessarily experiencing the reality those actions should express.

Heaven's culture operates by completely different principles. It values authenticity over appearance, transformation over conformity, and genuine connection over religious performance. It creates spaces where people can be honest about their struggles rather than hiding behind spiritual masks. It measures growth by increasing capacity to receive and transmit divine life rather than by religious activities or moral achievements.

The gap between religious moralism and heaven's culture explains why many spiritually hungry people find more life outside religious institutions than within them. They discover that breaking free from performance-based spirituality often creates space for genuine divine connection that religious systems unintentionally block. They learn that heaven values honest seekers more than perfect performers.

This doesn't mean moral behavior has no value. Ethics matter. Disciplines help. spiritual practices can create space for divine encounter. But these things must remain means rather than ends. The moment our focus shifts from connecting with divine life to perfecting our religious performance, we've exchanged the living reality for a lifeless substitute.

The culture of heaven consistently prioritizes transformation over behavior modification. It works from the inside out, changing desires rather than just controlling actions. It produces genuine fruit rather than manufactured results. It flows from divine initiative rather than human effort. Most importantly, it creates people who reflect heaven's nature because they've experienced heaven's life, not because they've mastered heaven's rules.

Recognizing Divine Fingerprints

If human goodness and religious performance can so closely mimic divine activity, how can we tell the difference? How do we know when we're experiencing the real thing rather than a convincing counterfeit? Heaven's genuine work carries distinct markers that set it apart from even the best human efforts. Learning to recognize these divine fingerprints develops our spiritual discernment.

First, heaven's work consistently bypasses human logic. It rarely follows the most obvious or reasonable path to a solution. Instead, it often takes unexpected detours that make no sense until we see the results. Divine strategies frequently appear foolish or inefficient from a human perspective. They target root causes we didn't even know existed.

They address problems from angles we would never consider. This counter-intuitive quality separates genuine divine activity from human goodness, which typically follows logical, straightforward approaches to solving problems.

Think about how water flows. Human engineering creates straight channels with right angles and predictable paths. Natural water finds unexpected routes, flowing around obstacles, seeping through tiny cracks, and gradually reshaping even the hardest stone. Divine activity resembles natural water flow more than human engineering. It follows organic patterns that human planning would never design but that ultimately prove more effective at reaching their destination.

Second, heaven's work produces disproportionate results from small inputs. When divine activity drives a process, the outcomes consistently exceed what the visible resources should be able to produce. Small acts of obedience create ripple effects far beyond their apparent significance. Limited resources multiply to meet expanding needs. Tiny beginnings grow into movements that transform entire communities. This multiplication effect distinguishes heaven's work from human goodness, which typically produces results proportional to the effort and resources invested.

Consider how seeds work. A tiny acorn contains no visible evidence of the massive oak tree it will become. Yet given the right conditions, that small seed produces results thousands of times larger than itself. Divine activity follows this seed principle, regularly producing harvest that far exceeds what the small beginning would suggest possible.

Third, heaven's work creates unusual unity among diverse people. When genuine divine activity drives a movement, it brings together individuals and groups that would normally remain separate or even opposed to each other. People from different backgrounds, generations, educational levels, and social classes find themselves drawn into surprising collaboration. Traditional barriers between groups become permeable or disappear entirely. This supernatural unity distinguishes heaven's work from human goodness, which typically brings together like-minded people but struggles to bridge significant social and cultural divides.

Think about how natural ecosystems function. Vastly different organisms— from microscopic bacteria to massive trees—work together in complex relationships that benefit the entire system. Divine activity creates similar spiritual ecosystems where diverse individuals and groups form interdependent networks that accomplish what none could do alone.

Fourth, heaven's work generates supernatural joy even in difficult circumstances. When divine activity drives a process, participants experience a quality of joy that transcends their situation. This isn't superficial happiness that depends on everything going well. It's a deeper gladness that persists even through challenges, setbacks, and opposition. This supernatural joy distinguishes heaven's work from human goodness, which typically produces satisfaction when things go well but struggles to maintain positive emotional states when facing significant obstacles.

Consider how certain plants thrive in conditions that would kill most vegetation. Desert flowers bloom after years of drought. Arctic plants grow in freezing temperatures. Similarly, divine joy flourishes in circumstances where human happiness would wither and die. This counterintuitive emotional flourishing marks authentic heaven-originated activity.

DEVELOPING SPIRITUAL TASTE BUDS

Discernment between human goodness and divine activity isn't primarily intellectual. You can't master it just by memorizing a list of differences. It's more like developing a palate that can distinguish fine wine from grape juice. It requires experience, practice, and attention to subtle qualities that casual observers miss.

Think about how wine experts work. They don't just read about different wines. They taste them. They pay attention to subtle notes and flavors that most people never notice. They compare different varieties and vintages. They train their senses to detect nuances that reveal the quality, origin, and character of each wine they sample. spiritual discernment works the same way. It develops through direct experience with both human goodness and divine activity, learning to detect the distinct "flavor" of each.

This experiential approach to discernment explains why some people with limited theological education often recognize genuine divine activity more quickly than religious scholars. They've developed spiritual taste buds through direct experience rather than abstract knowledge. They know the flavor of heaven's presence because they've tasted it repeatedly, not because they can define it intellectually.

You can train your spiritual senses to recognize the authentic flavor of heaven's presence. This training happens through repeated exposure to genuine divine activity followed by thoughtful reflection on what you experienced. Each encounter with heaven's reality refines your ability to distinguish it from even the most convincing counterfeits.

Start by paying attention to the aftertaste of different spiritual experiences. Human goodness, including religious performance, often leaves a subtle aftertaste of pride, exhaustion, or emptiness once the initial satisfaction fades. Divine activity leaves a distinctly different aftertaste—a lingering sense of wonder, deep peace, and renewed energy that actually increases rather than decreases with time.

Notice how different spiritual activities affect your sense of identity. Human goodness, especially religious performance, subtly reinforces self-importance. It makes you feel better about yourself because of what you've accomplished. Divine activity does the opposite. It creates a healthy self-forgetfulness where your attention shifts from your own spiritual status to the beauty and goodness you've encountered. You think less about how the experience reflects on you and more about what it reveals about divine reality.

Pay attention to how different approaches affect your relationship with others. Human goodness, particularly religious varieties, often creates subtle comparison and competition. You notice who's doing more or less than you are. You feel superior to those who aren't as active or committed. Divine activity generates a completely different social effect. It produces genuine humility that sees others more clearly and values them more deeply. It creates connections based on shared wonder rather than shared performance.

Most importantly, notice the fruit that different activities produce in your life and community. Human goodness generates temporary improvements that require constant maintenance. Divine activity creates lasting transformation that continues to develop and spread even without ongoing human effort. Human goodness addresses visible symptoms. Divine activity heals root causes that human wisdom often fails to identify. Human goodness helps people cope with broken systems. Divine activity transforms the systems themselves.

As you practice this kind of attentive discernment, you'll develop increasingly sensitive spiritual taste buds. You'll recognize the flavor of genuine divine activity more quickly and accurately. You'll spot even sophisticated counterfeits that fool most observers. Most importantly, you'll develop a hunger for the real thing that makes you unwilling to settle for even the most impressive substitutes.

Recap: Sharpening Your Discernment

You've discovered how human goodness can counterfeit divine activity. Kind acts, positive thinking, and moral behavior that originate from our best intentions rather than divine direction often become the most effective barriers to genuine transformation. They create a substitute that looks so much like the real thing that most people never recognize the difference.

You've learned why religious performance actually blocks heaven's culture. The pursuit of being "good Christians" or "good spiritual people" can immunize us against authentic divine life by satisfying our spiritual hunger just enough to prevent us from seeking the real thing. Religious moralism substitutes external conformity for internal transformation, creating spiritual performers rather than genuine participants in divine reality.

You've explored the distinct markers of genuine divine work. Heaven's activity consistently bypasses human logic, produces disproportionate results from small inputs, creates unusual unity among diverse people, and generates supernatural joy even in difficult circumstances. These divine fingerprints help you distinguish authentic heaven-originated transformation from even the most impressive human counterfeits.

You've discovered that discernment between human goodness and divine activity isn't primarily intellectual but experiential. Like developing a palate that can distinguish fine wine from grape juice, you can train your spiritual senses to recognize the authentic flavor of heaven's presence through direct experience and thoughtful reflection.

Now it's time to put this understanding into practice. Start by examining your current spiritual activities to identify what's merely good versus what's truly God initiated. Look at your religious practices, service activities, and spiritual disciplines. Ask yourself: Am I doing these things primarily from my own determination to be a good person? Or am I responding to specific divine guidance? The answer reveals whether you're experiencing human goodness or divine activity.

Practice saying no to religious obligations that lack divine life. This doesn't mean abandoning all structure or commitment. It means becoming more selective about where you invest your spiritual energy. Choose depth over breadth. Quality over quantity. Divine guidance over human expectations. Learn to recognize the subtle pressure to perform religiously and consciously resist it in favor of genuine connection with divine reality.

Document experiences that carried the unmistakable markers of heaven. When have you seen counter-intuitive approaches produce unexpected breakthroughs? When have small inputs created disproportionate results? When have diverse people come together in unusual unity? When have you experienced supernatural joy despite difficult circumstances? these experiences form reference points that help you recognize divine activity more quickly in the future.

Intentionally expose yourself to environments where authentic divine activity is happening. Seek out people and communities that show evidence of heaven's fingerprints rather than just impressive religious programs. Pay attention to how these environments feel different from spaces dominated by human goodness or religious performance. Notice how they affect your spiritual hunger, your sense of identity, and your relationship with others.

Share your discernment journey with trusted companions who are asking similar questions. Comparing notes with others helps sharpen your perception and confirms patterns you might miss on your own. It also creates accountability that prevents you from settling for comfortable counterfeits when genuine divine activity challenges your preferences or assumptions.

Remember that developing spiritual discernment takes time. Don't expect perfect clarity immediately. Like any skill, it grows through practice, mistakes, and gradual refinement. Be patient with yourself as you learn to distinguish between what's merely good and what's genuinely God - initiated. Each step in this journey increases your capacity to recognize and participate in heaven's transformative work on earth.

The divine discernment crisis represents one of the most significant spiritual challenges of our time. In a world filled with human goodness and religious activity, learning to recognize and respond to genuine divine initiative separates those who merely improve their circumstances from those who experience supernatural transformation. As you develop this critical discernment, you'll find yourself increasingly able to participate in heaven's culture rather than just producing more human goodness.

The stakes couldn't be higher. When we mistake human goodness for divine activity, we settle for far less than heaven offers. We exhaust ourselves trying to produce through effort what can only come through divine life. We create temporary improvements instead of lasting transformation. But when we learn to recognize and respond to genuine divine initiative, we become channels for supernatural power that changes not just individual lives but entire systems and cultures.

Your growing ability to discern between good and God positions you as a genuine agent of heaven's culture on earth. Not because you've mastered religious performance or achieved moral perfection, but because you've learned to recognize and respond to divine activity that transforms from the inside out rather than conforming from the outside in. This discernment makes you dangerous to systems of darkness precisely because you can no longer be satisfied with counterfeits, no matter how impressive they appear.

The Five Invasion Tactics: Heaven's Infiltration Methods

Divine Coincidence Chains

Most people think coincidences are just random events. You bump into an old friend at the grocery store. Someone mentions a book title just as you were thinking about it. You get a job offer the day after praying about your finances. We call these things coincidences because they seem unplanned. But what if they're not random at all? What if these moments are actually carefully designed connections in a divine strategy to transform your life and the world around you?

Heaven uses a powerful invasion tactic called divine coincidence chains. These are series of seemingly random events that connect in ways that create supernatural impact. One small coincidence leads to another, then another, until something happens that changes everything. Like dominoes set up in a perfect line, each small event triggers the next until the final domino falls and completes a picture no one could see at the beginning.

Think about how water forms canyons. It doesn't happen all at once with one big flood. It happens drop by drop, day after day, year after year. Each drop seems tiny and insignificant, but together over time, they carve massive changes in solid rock. Divine coincidence chains work the same way. Each small connection might seem meaningless on its own, but together they create changes that no human plan could achieve.

I met a woman named Sarah who lost her job unexpectedly. The very next day, her car broke down. Then her landlord raised her rent. Everything seemed to be falling apart at once. But these apparent disasters forced her to move in temporarily with an elderly neighbor who needed help around the house. During that time, Sarah discovered she had a gift for elder care. A visitor to the neighbor's home noticed Sarah's natural abilities and mentioned a new community program starting up. Today, Sarah runs a thriving elder care network that serves hundreds of seniors. What looked like random bad luck was actually a divine coincidence chain positioning her exactly where she needed to be.

The power of divine coincidence chains is that they bypass human limitations. They don't depend on your resources, connections, or abilities. They work through ordinary events that anyone might experience. The key difference is recognizing these events as connected rather than random. When you start seeing coincidences as potential divine connections, you begin to respond differently. You pay more attention. You stay curious. You follow the trail of "random" events to see where they might lead.

These chains often start with something so small you might easily miss it. A thought that pops into your mind about someone you haven't seen in years. An article that catches your eye for no apparent reason. A wrong turn that puts you on an unfamiliar street. These tiny moments become the first links in chains that can eventually transform families, heal communities, and sometimes even change the course of history.

Heaven designs these chains to accomplish things that human planning never could. They connect people who would never normally meet. They bring together resources that seemed impossible to find. They create solutions to problems that appeared unsolvable. And they do it all through events so ordinary that most people never recognize the divine strategy operating right under their noses.

Prophetic Disruption

Have you ever had someone say something to you that stopped you in your tracks? Maybe it was just a simple comment, but it hit you at exactly the right moment and changed how you saw everything. That's prophetic disruption in action.

Prophetic disruption happens when small, divinely-inspired words or actions break through established patterns of thinking and behaving.

These moments create tiny cracks in mental walls that have kept people trapped in limited perspectives. They interrupt negative thought cycles that have run on repeat for years. They challenge assumptions so basic that people didn't even know they were making them.

Unlike big, dramatic confrontations that cause people to become defensive, prophetic disruptions are usually gentle and often indirect. They slip past mental guards because they don't look threatening. A child asks an innocent question that exposes flawed logic. A friend makes an offhand comment that suddenly illuminates a blind spot. A stranger says something that seems random but addresses exactly what you've been struggling with privately.

I know a business leader who ran his company with an iron fist for twenty years. His employees feared him. Turnover was high. Despite financial success, the workplace culture was toxic. One day, his four-year-old granddaughter visited his office and asked innocently, "Grandpa, why is everyone here so sad?" That simple question from a child pierced his heart in a way that no employee feedback, consultant report, or board meeting ever had. It began a transformation that eventually changed the entire company culture.

The power of prophetic disruption comes from its precision. Heaven knows exactly where the cracks in our thinking are—the vulnerable points where a small word can create an opening for new perspective. Like acupuncture that targets specific points to release healing throughout the body, prophetic disruption applies gentle pressure at exactly the right spot to release mental and emotional blockages that have prevented transformation.

These disruptive moments often come through the most unexpected sources. Children. Strangers. People outside your social circle or expertise. This is strategic, not accidental. When insights come from unexpected sources, they bypass our normal filters and defenses. We can't easily dismiss them based on the speaker's credentials or our history with them. The very unexpectedness of the source creates space for the message to land.

Prophetic disruptions don't always feel spiritual when they happen. They rarely come with dramatic signs or religious language. They arrive embedded in ordinary conversations and everyday interactions. Their power isn't in their delivery but in their perfect timing and precise content. They address exactly what you need to hear, exactly when you need to hear it, in exactly the way you're able to receive it.

Heaven uses this tactic to create openings where rigid thinking has created barriers to transformation. In workplaces where toxic cultures have become normalized. In families where unhealthy patterns have persisted for generations. In communities where prejudice has hardened into unquestioned assumptions. In religious groups where traditions have replaced living connection with divine reality. These environments resist frontal assault but remain vulnerable to small, precise disruptions that create cracks where new life can enter.

Stealth Compassion

Many people have built up strong walls against anything that seems religious. They've been hurt by hypocritical believers. They've seen spiritual language used to manipulate and control. They've developed automatic defenses against anything that sounds like preaching or proselytizing. These walls make perfect sense as protection against past wounds. But they also block genuine divine connection that could bring healing and transformation.

Heaven's response to these defenses isn't to attack them directly or argue against them. Instead, it deploys a powerful invasion tactic called stealth compassion. This approach delivers acts of kindness and practical help in ways that bypass skepticism and religious prejudice. These acts create experiences of divine love that transform recipients before they can activate their intellectual resistance.

Stealth compassion works because it separates the experience of divine love from the religious packaging that has created negative associations. It delivers the substance without the labels that trigger defenses. Like a medicine delivered in a form the body won't reject, these acts of kindness slip past mental barriers and touch hearts that have become inaccessible to more direct approaches.

I know a man named James who had rejected all religion after being deeply hurt by a church in his youth. His defenses were impenetrable when it came to anything spiritual. During a difficult time in his life, anonymous gifts began appearing on his doorstep. Groceries when his cupboards were bare. Gas cards when his tank was empty. Notes of encouragement that somehow addressed exactly what he was going through without being preachy. For months this continued, and James never discovered who was behind it. The experience of being known and cared for so specifically began to soften his heart toward the possibility that divine love might be real, even if religious institutions had failed him.

The power of stealth compassion comes from its anonymity and unexpectedness. When people can't identify a human source for the kindness they're receiving, they're more likely to consider supernatural possibilities. When help arrives in forms they never requested but that perfectly meet their needs, it creates questions that intellectual defenses can't easily answer. Who knew exactly what I needed? How did this arrive at precisely the right moment? Why would someone help me without wanting recognition?

This tactic is especially effective with people who have been wounded by religious hypocrisy. They've developed strong antibodies against spiritual language and religious approaches. But they remain vulnerable to genuine love expressed in practical ways. Their defenses are designed to repel preachers but have no response prepared for anonymous kindness that asks nothing in return.

Stealth compassion doesn't manipulate or trick people. It simply creates experiences of divine love without the religious packaging that has created negative associations. It gives people space to experience the reality before they have to deal with the labels. It allows them to encounter divine care directly rather than through the distorting lens of religious systems that may have hurt them in the past.

Heaven uses this tactic to reach people who would never enter a church building, read a spiritual book, or engage in a religious conversation. It creates evidence of divine love that skeptics can't easily dismiss because it addresses needs they've never spoken aloud. It demonstrates supernatural knowledge and timing without making claims that trigger intellectual resistance. It shows rather than tells, creating experiences that raise questions materialistic worldviews struggle to answer.

Strategic Joyful Presence

Walk into any room filled with anxious, stressed, or conflicted people. Now imagine one person who carries a genuine sense of peace and joy that doesn't depend on the circumstances. Watch how the atmosphere begins to shift around them. This isn't just a psychological phenomenon. It's a spiritual reality that heaven strategically deploys as an invasion tactic.

Strategic joyful presence happens when heaven releases supernatural joy and peace through ordinary people in environments dominated by anxiety, conflict, or despair. This creates a contagious atmosphere that shifts the spiritual climate without a single word being spoken. Like walking into a room filled with the smell of freshbaked bread, this presence affects everyone who enters its radius.

Unlike forced positivity or superficial happiness, this joy has depth and substance that people can sense immediately. It doesn't deny problems or pain. It transcends them. It doesn't depend on everything going well. It persists even in difficult circumstances. This quality makes it immediately distinguishable from normal human emotions that rise and fall based on external conditions.

I know a woman who works in a high-stress corporate environment where burnout and backstabbing are normal. She isn't the CEO or even a manager. She's an administrative assistant with no formal authority. Yet her cubicle has become an unofficial oasis where people from throughout the company stop by when they're having a rough day. She doesn't counsel them or preach to them. She simply carries a presence that somehow helps people breathe easier and see more clearly. Several executives have privately admitted that her cubicle is the one place in the building where they can think straight when facing difficult decisions.

The power of strategic joyful presence comes from its inexplicability. When someone remains genuinely peaceful and joyful in circumstances that should produce stress and anxiety, it creates a cognitive dissonance that opens minds to new possibilities. People naturally wonder: What does this person know that I don't? What source are they connected to that I'm missing? How can I experience what they're experiencing?

This tactic works especially well in environments where words have lost their impact. Workplaces where people have become cynical about mission statements and corporate values. Families where the same arguments have played out so many times that no one listens anymore. Communities where opposing groups have hardened into positions that make dialogue impossible. In these settings, a presence that embodies an alternative reality speaks louder than any words could.

The joyful presence tactic doesn't require special training or techniques. It simply needs people who have experienced genuine divine joy and peace to bring that reality with them into environments that operate according to different values. The contrast between the atmosphere they carry and the prevailing climate creates a disturbance in the status quo that makes space for new possibilities to emerge.

Heaven deploys this tactic strategically, positioning people in specific environments where their presence will have maximum impact. The peaceful parent in a neighborhood known for domestic conflict. The joyful teacher in a school plagued by discouragement. The genuinely happy service worker in a business where customer interactions are typically tense. These placements aren't random. They're strategic insertions of heaven's atmosphere into places that desperately need an alternative to the prevailing spiritual climate.

Value-System Infiltration

Every culture operates according to unwritten rules and values that determine what gets rewarded, what gets punished, and what seems normal to the people within it. These value systems shape behavior more powerfully than laws or policies ever could. They create the invisible framework that guides daily decisions and interactions without most people even realizing it's there.

Heaven's fifth invasion tactic targets these cultural value systems directly. Value-system infiltration happens when heaven's priorities quietly replace cultural values in specific environments through people who embody a different way of living. This creates alternative communities within the larger culture that demonstrate the superior results of operating according to heaven's values.

Unlike direct confrontation that triggers defensive reactions, value-system infiltration works through consistent demonstration of a better alternative. It doesn't attack existing values with arguments or criticism. It simply establishes working models that produce results the current system cannot achieve. The evidence of these results gradually undermines confidence in the prevailing values and creates curiosity about the alternative.

I know a couple who started a small business in an industry known for cutthroat competition and questionable ethics. Instead of adopting the prevailing values, they built their company on radical honesty with customers, unusual generosity toward employees, and genuine care for competitors. Industry insiders predicted quick failure. Ten years later, their business has become one of the most successful in their region. More importantly, several competitors have begun adopting similar practices after seeing the results. The value system of an entire industry is slowly shifting because one small company demonstrated a better alternative.

The power of value-system infiltration comes from its focus on results rather than rhetoric. It doesn't just claim that heaven's values work better; it proves it by creating visible outcomes that the current system cannot produce. Happy families in neighborhoods where dysfunction is normal. Thriving businesses in industries where ethical corners are typically cut. Reconciled relationships in communities divided by long-standing conflicts. These tangible results speak louder than any argument could.

This tactic works because humans naturally move toward what produces life and flourishing. When people see genuine joy, peace, and abundance flowing from a different set of values than the ones they've accepted as normal, curiosity naturally follows. This curiosity creates openings for value transfer that no amount of preaching or teaching could achieve. People don't need to be convinced theoretically that heaven's values work better; they can see the evidence with their own eyes.

Value-system infiltration targets the most influential domains of culture: families, workplaces, entertainment, education, and community life. By establishing outposts of heaven's culture within these domains, it creates accessible models that others can observe and eventually imitate. Each successful model becomes a seed that can spread heaven's values throughout its surrounding environment.

Heaven deploys this tactic with remarkable patience. It doesn't expect immediate total transformation of entire cultures. It works incrementally, establishing small outposts that gradually expand their influence. Like yeast working through dough, these alternative communities slowly transform their surroundings by demonstrating the superior results of operating according to heaven's values rather than cultural defaults.

Implementing Heaven's Tactics

Now that you understand the five invasion tactics heaven uses to transform earth, how do you put them into practice? How do you move from understanding these methods to actually implementing them in your daily life? The good news is that participation doesn't require special training or supernatural abilities. It simply requires recognition and response.

Start by paying attention to coincidences in your life. Those "random" connections and timing that seem too perfect to be accidental might actually be the first links in divine coincidence chains. Begin documenting these moments in a journal. Note when you bump into someone unexpectedly and the conversation addresses exactly what you've been thinking about. Record when opportunities arise that connect perfectly with previous events in ways you couldn't have planned. Look for patterns in these coincidences. They often reveal divine strategies unfolding in your life.

When you notice potential divine coincidences, respond to them rather than dismissing them. Follow the trail of "random" connections to see where they lead. Call the person who came to mind unexpectedly. Explore the opportunity that appeared out of nowhere. Accept the invitation that doesn't fit your normal routine. Each response potentially activates the next link in a chain that could lead to progresss far beyond what you can currently imagine.

Practice delivering small words of encouragement that might serve as prophetic disruptions in someone's life. You don't need to be dramatic or use spiritual language. Simple observations offered at the right moment can create openings where new perspectives can enter. "I notice you're really good at bringing people together." "That comment you made in the meeting showed unusual wisdom." "Have you ever considered that your struggle might actually be preparing you for something important?" These gentle observations can interrupt negative thought patterns and create space for new possibilities.

Pay attention to inner promptings about specific needs people might have, even if they haven't expressed them. Then find ways to meet those needs anonymously or unexpectedly. Leave a gift card with an encouraging note on a coworker's desk. Send a meal to a family going through a tough time. Put cash in an envelope for someone you know is struggling financially. Don't sign your name or seek recognition. Let the experience of being cared for specifically and mysteriously do its work without religious explanation or personal credit.

Cultivate genuine joy and peace that doesn't depend on circumstances. This isn't about faking positive emotions or denying real problems. It's about connecting with a source of joy beyond your situation. Spend time in practices that strengthen this connection—whether that's prayer, meditation, time in nature, or whatever helps you experience divine presence personally. Then intentionally bring this authentic joy into environments dominated by anxiety, conflict, or despair. Don't preach or explain. Simply be a carrier of an alternative atmosphere.

Identify one cultural value you can subvert through your lifestyle choices. Maybe it's the value of busy-ness as a status symbol. Perhaps it's the assumption that success requires stepping on others. Or the belief that accumulating possessions brings happiness. Choose to live visibly by a different value and let the results speak for themselves. Don't criticize those who live by cultural defaults. Simply demonstrate a compelling alternative that produces visibly better outcomes.

Remember that implementing these tactics doesn't require grand gestures or dramatic confrontations. Heaven's invasion strategy works through small, consistent actions that accumulate over time. The power comes not from the impressiveness of any single act but from the compound effect of many small acts aligned with divine purposes.

Start where you are with what you have. You don't need a platform, resources, or influence to begin. Some of heaven's most effective agents are people with no impressive credentials or visible authority. Their impact comes not from their position but from their precise alignment with divine strategy. A small action perfectly positioned often accomplishes more than grand efforts in the wrong place or time.

Pay attention to the results of implementing these tactics. Notice how divine coincidence chains create connections no human could orchestrate. Observe how small prophetic disruptions create openings in seemingly impenetrable mindsets. Watch how stealth compassion bypasses defenses that direct approaches could never penetrate. See how strategic joyful presence shifts atmospheres without a word being spoken. Document how value-system infiltration gradually transforms environments from the inside out.

These observations will strengthen your confidence in heaven's invasion strategy and sharpen your ability to participate effectively. They'll help you recognize divine patterns more quickly and respond more precisely. Most importantly, they'll free you from dependency on human methods that may look impressive but lack the transformative power of heaven's seemingly simple tactics.

As you implement these methods, remain flexible and responsive rather than rigid and formulaic. Heaven's invasion tactics follow patterns but never become mechanical formulas. They require ongoing sensitivity to divine guidance rather than rote application of techniques. What worked perfectly in one situation may need adjustment in another. The key is maintaining connection with the divine intelligence coordinating the larger strategy rather than simply repeating methods that worked previously.

Finally, connect with others who are implementing these same tactics in their spheres of influence. Not to create a new organization or program, but to share insights, encourage each other, and occasionally collaborate when your assignments overlap. These connections create synergy that multiplies effectiveness beyond what any individual could achieve alone. They also provide confirmation and clarity when you're unsure about the patterns you're seeing or the promptings you're receiving.

The five invasion tactics—divine coincidence chains, prophetic disruption, stealth compassion, strategic joyful presence, and value-system infiltration— provide a practical framework for participating in heaven's transformation of earth. They don't require special status, extensive training, or impressive spiritual credentials. They simply need people who recognize divine patterns and respond to divine promptings in the ordinary moments of daily life.

As you implement these tactics consistently, you'll find yourself becoming an increasingly effective agent of heaven's culture on earth. Not because you've mastered complex spiritual techniques, but because you've learned to align with a divine strategy that has been transforming reality since the beginning of time. You'll discover that your seemingly small acts of obedience form part of a sophisticated campaign that is systematically dismantling systems of darkness and establishing outposts of heaven's culture throughout the earth.

The invasion is already underway. Heaven's culture is already infiltrating earth through ordinary people who have recognized and responded to divine strategy. Now it's your turn to join this quiet revolution that is changing everything one coincidence chain, one disruptive word, one anonymous act of kindness, one joyful presence, and one subverted value system at a time.

The Four Components of Heaven's Culture

Component 1: Faith in the Divine

Heaven's culture starts with something simple but powerful - trust. Not the kind of trust you put in a sturdy chair or a friend who keeps secrets. This is a deep, lifechanging trust in something bigger than yourself. It's believing that divine goodness and power are real, even when you can't see them working.

Most people think faith means following religious rules or saying the right prayers. They see it as something you do at special buildings on certain days of the week. But real faith in the divine goes way beyond that. It's not about checking boxes or performing rituals. It's about having a genuine relationship with God that changes how you see everything else.

Think about how you trust gravity without thinking about it. You don't wake up wondering if you'll float away today. You simply live your life knowing gravity will keep working. Faith in the divine works like that when it's real. It becomes the background reality that shapes all your other thoughts and actions. You stop questioning whether God exists or cares about you, and you start living from the settled conviction that divine love and power are the most real things in your life.

This kind of trust doesn't come from trying harder to believe. It grows through experiences where you see divine goodness show up in your life. Maybe it was that time when help arrived just when you needed it most. Or when you felt a peace that made no sense given what was happening around you. Or when you followed a strange prompt and it led to something amazing you could never have planned. These moments build your trust muscle over time.

When faith in the divine becomes real, it changes everything else. Your work becomes more than just earning money - it becomes a place to express divine love and creativity. Your relationships shift from what you can get to what you can give. Your problems look different because you see them against the backdrop of a bigger story where good ultimately wins.

The culture of heaven runs on this kind of faith. Not religious obligation that drains life from you, but genuine trust that fills you with energy and hope. People who carry heaven's culture might not use religious language or attend religious services. But they have this unshakable trust that shapes how they move through the world.

I met a woman named Maria who cleaned hotel rooms for a living. She had no impressive religious title or platform. But she carried this remarkable faith that transformed her simple job into something powerful. She prayed over each room she cleaned, believing that divine peace would touch whoever stayed there next. Hotel guests would specifically request rooms she had cleaned, saying they slept better there, though they had no idea why. Her faith wasn't just a private belief - it created ripples of heaven's culture that others could feel.

Faith in the divine works best when it's both deeply personal and practically expressed. It's not just believing certain facts about God in your head. It's trusting divine goodness so completely that it changes how you treat the cashier at the grocery store, how you handle disappointment, and how you view people who disagree with you.

This component of heaven's culture stands in sharp contrast to both religious performance and secular materialism. Religious performance says, "Follow these rules and God will accept you." Secular materialism says, "There is no divine reality beyond what we can measure." Faith in the divine says, "Divine love is the most real thing in the universe, and it's already reaching toward you."

When a community of people begins to live from this kind of faith, something shifts in the atmosphere around them. Problems that seemed impossible start to look different. Resources appear from unexpected places. Relationships heal in ways that defy explanation. The invisible reality of divine goodness begins to become visible through ordinary people who simply trust it's real.

Component 2: Heavenly Priorities

Every culture has a value system that determines what people chase after, celebrate, and sacrifice for. In most earthly cultures, the priorities are pretty clear: get more money, gain more status, look more attractive, accumulate more stuff, and protect yourself from those who might take what you have.

Heaven's culture operates on completely different priorities. Success looks nothing like what you see in magazines or on social media. In heaven's culture, the most successful person isn't the one with the biggest house or the most followers online. It's the one who loves most genuinely, helps others most effectively, and stays most connected to divine presence.

This difference in priorities changes everything about how people live. In earth's cultures, you work hard to get ahead of others. In heaven's culture, you work hard to lift others up. In earth's cultures, you protect what's yours. In heaven's culture, you share freely, knowing there's always more where that came from. In earth's cultures, you try to look perfect. In heaven's culture, you embrace your flaws as spaces where divine light can shine through.

The priorities of heaven flip our normal thinking upside down. Things we usually chase turn out not to matter much at all. Things we often ignore turn out to be incredibly valuable. It's like discovering that you've been collecting plastic beads while walking past real diamonds without noticing them.

Take money, for example. Earth's cultures teach us that gathering more money means greater success and security. Heaven's culture sees money as a tool for creating blessing, not as a measure of worth or a source of safety. People who live by heaven's priorities still work hard and handle money wisely, but they hold it loosely, always ready to share when they see genuine need.

Or consider status and recognition. Earth's cultures push us to build our personal brand and get more followers, likes, and praise. Heaven's culture values hidden service that may never be recognized publicly. The person quietly caring for a sick neighbor might rank higher in heaven's value system than the celebrity getting applause on stage.

Even religious activities get reprioritized. Earth's religious cultures often value church attendance, Bible knowledge, and moral rule-following above all else. Heaven's culture values transformed hearts that naturally produce love, joy, peace, patience, kindness, goodness, faithfulness, gentleness, and self-control. You can do all the religious activities perfectly and still miss the priorities that matter most.

I know a businessman who discovered heaven's priorities midway through a successful career. He had followed the normal path - working long hours, climbing the corporate ladder, accumulating wealth. But something felt empty. Through a series of unexpected encounters, he began to see a different way of measuring success. Today, he still runs his company, but with completely different priorities. He measures growth not just in profits but in how many employees find purpose in their work. He sees his resources not as personal security but as tools for creating opportunity for others. His definition of a "good day" has nothing to do with stock prices and everything to do with whether love was expressed and people were valued.

Living by heaven's priorities doesn't mean becoming poor or unsuccessful by earthly standards. Many people who align with heaven's value system thrive financially and professionally. The difference is in how they define success and what they do with whatever resources and influence they gain. They hold earthly rewards loosely while gripping heavenly values tightly.

The shift to heaven's priorities rarely happens all at once. It usually begins in one area of life and gradually spreads to others. You might start seeing your time differently, becoming more generous with it toward people in need. Then you notice your attitude toward money changing. Then your view of success at work shifts.

Before long, you're operating on a completely different value system than those around you.

This component of heaven's culture is perhaps the most countercultural of all. It directly challenges the core assumptions that drive most human societies. It questions what we chase, how we measure worth, and what we consider valuable. It offers an alternative way of living that looks foolish by worldly standards but produces a quality of life that money can't buy and status can't deliver.

When a community begins living by heaven's priorities, it creates a stark contrast with the surrounding culture. People notice the difference. They may not immediately understand or embrace these different priorities, but they can't help seeing that something unusual is happening. This visible contrast becomes an invitation to consider whether there might be a better way to live than the one they've always known.

Component 3: Divine Revelation

Imagine trying to navigate a city using only your own observations and guesses. No maps, no GPS, no asking locals for directions. You might eventually find your way around, but you'd waste a lot of time and energy taking wrong turns. That's how many people live their entire lives - trying to figure things out using only their limited human perspective.

Heaven's culture offers something radically different: direct access to divine insight about yourself, others, and situations you face. This isn't about having all the answers or never making mistakes. It's about living with a continuous flow of guidance that comes from beyond your own thinking.

Divine revelation isn't just for special religious leaders or prophets in ancient stories. It's available to anyone who learns how to recognize and respond to it. It comes through many channels - sometimes through scripture that suddenly speaks directly to your situation, sometimes through dreams that contain wisdom you couldn't have invented, sometimes through thoughts that drop into your mind with a different quality than your normal thinking.

This component of heaven's culture transforms decision-making from educated guessing to guided partnership. Instead of weighing pros and cons and hoping for the best, you learn to recognize divine nudges that often point in unexpected directions. These nudges might contradict conventional wisdom or challenge your natural inclinations, but they consistently lead to better outcomes than you could have planned on your own.

I know a teacher who was facing a particularly difficult student. She had tried every technique in her training without success. One morning while praying, she felt a clear impression to ask the boy about his artwork, though she hadn't even known he was interested in art. That simple question, which came from beyond her own strategy, opened a door. She discovered he had extraordinary artistic talent that had never been recognized. Their relationship transformed, and his behavior in class completely changed. No educational theory would have prescribed her approach. It came from divine revelation tailored specifically to that unique situation.

This kind of revelation often contradicts what seems logical. It might tell you to take a job that pays less when you need more money. It might prompt you to trust someone that others warn you about. It might direct you to start a project that seems destined to fail. Following these divine nudges requires courage because they rarely make complete sense at the time. The full picture only becomes clear in retrospect, when you see how each piece fits into a plan you couldn't have designed yourself.

Living by divine revelation doesn't mean you stop using your brain or ignore wise counsel from others. It means you add another dimension to your decision making process. You still gather information, consider options, and seek advice. But you also tune in to impressions, promptings, and insights that come from beyond your natural thinking.

This component of heaven's culture creates people who consistently make choices that don't make sense by normal standards but produce extraordinary results. They take risks that seem foolish but lead to advancementss. They invest in people that others have given up on. They pursue solutions that experts dismiss. Their lives have a sense of divine coordination that goes beyond good planning or positive thinking.

Learning to recognize divine revelation takes practice. It's like developing any skill - you get better with experience. At first, you might question whether an impression is really from God or just your own thoughts. You might follow a prompting and find it doesn't work out as you expected. But over time, you learn to distinguish the unique quality of divine guidance from your own wishes or fears.

The culture of heaven runs on this continuous access to divine perspective. People who live in this reality make decisions differently, solve problems differently, and relate to others differently than those limited to human wisdom alone. They live with a sense of partnership with divine intelligence that guides their steps, often in unexpected but ultimately life-giving directions.

When a community begins operating by divine revelation, it develops an unusual ability to navigate complex situations with wisdom that surprises outside observers. Problems that stump experts suddenly find solutions. Conflicts that seemed irresolvable find paths to reconciliation. Resources appear precisely when needed. The community becomes known for a kind of guidance that goes beyond human strategy and consistently produces results that defy conventional explanation.

Component 4: Kingdom Norms

Every culture has unwritten rules about how people should behave. These norms shape daily life more powerfully than official laws or policies. They determine what feels normal, what seems strange, and what gets rejected as completely unacceptable. Most people follow these unwritten rules without even thinking about them.

Heaven's culture establishes a completely different set of norms than those that govern earthly societies. These kingdom norms aren't rigid religious rules that squeeze the life out of people. They're life-giving patterns that create environments where divine reality can flourish naturally.

Take forgiveness, for example. In most cultures, forgiveness is conditional. You forgive if the other person deserves it, if they apologize properly, if they make appropriate amends. Heaven's culture practices radical forgiveness that doesn't depend on the other person's response. People forgive not primarily to benefit the offender but to free themselves from the poison of resentment and to break cycles of retaliation that have destroyed communities for generations.

Or consider generosity. Earth's cultures teach calculated giving based on what you can spare or what you'll get in return. Heaven's culture practices supernatural generosity that often makes no sense by normal accounting. People give beyond their apparent means, trusting that divine resources operate by different mathematics than human economies. They give without seeking recognition, sometimes anonymously, believing that the impact matters more than who gets credit.

Another kingdom norm is truthful speech. While many cultures normalize "little white lies" and strategic deception, heaven's culture values words that align with reality. This isn't harsh truth-telling that wounds others. It's speaking with both accuracy and love, addressing real issues without crushing the people involved. This commitment to truth creates environments of trust where genuine problems can be solved rather than covered up.

Perhaps the most countercultural norm is finding joy in suffering. Earth's cultures teach us to avoid discomfort at all costs and to complain when we can't escape it. Heaven's culture sees suffering as a potential pathway to growth and deeper connection with divine presence. People learn to find meaning and even joy in difficult seasons, not because the pain itself is good but because they discover treasures in darkness that they might have missed in easier times.

I know a family that lives by these kingdom norms in ways that puzzle their neighbors. When someone damaged their property, they responded with kindness rather than threats. When facing financial pressure, they continued giving generously to others in need. When confronted with terminal illness, they found ways to encourage the medical staff caring for them. These responses seem strange by normal standards, but they create a distinct atmosphere around this family that others find both challenging and attractive.

Kingdom norms aren't maintained through guilt or external pressure. They flow naturally from the other components of heaven's culture. When you trust divine goodness deeply, embrace heaven's priorities, and live by divine revelation, these patterns of behavior emerge organically. You forgive because you've experienced forgiveness. You give generously because you trust divine provision. You speak the truth because you value authentic relationships over appearance management.

These norms create environments where divine life flourishes naturally. Just as certain plants thrive in specific soil conditions, divine reality manifests most powerfully where these kingdom patterns are practiced consistently. The norms themselves don't create heaven's culture, but they provide the conditions where it can take root and spread.

Unlike rigid religious rules that focus on controlling external behavior, kingdom norms address the heart attitudes that produce behavior. They ask not just "What did you do?" but "Who are you becoming?" They recognize that lasting transformation happens from the inside out, not from the outside in. They value growth over pretending, recognizing that authenticity is more meaningful than maintaining a false image of perfection. In their view, every person is in a process of becoming—a journey where spiritual, emotional, and personal development unfolds over time. Rather than expecting immediate mastery or flawless behavior, they emphasize sincerity and the willingness to grow, understanding that true transformation occurs gradually.

Pretending, in this context, refers to putting on a façade—acting in ways that may appear righteous or ideal without actually being rooted in genuine inner change. This kind of pretense can create disconnection from oneself and from others. In contrast, growth involves humility, honesty, and openness to learning, which fosters lasting alignment with the deeper, divine patterns that shape a meaningful and spiritually authentic life. They believe that as individuals grow in self-awareness, love, and integrity, the expression of these divine qualities becomes more effortless and real—flowing naturally from who they are becoming, not from a role they are trying to play.

When a community begins practicing these kingdom norms together, it creates a culture that feels noticeably different from its surroundings. People who enter this environment often can't immediately identify what's different, but they sense a distinct atmosphere. There's more peace, more joy, more authenticity, more freedom than they typically experience. This atmosphere itself becomes an invitation to discover the divine reality that produced it.

Recap: Cultivating Heaven's Culture

You've now explored the four essential components that make up heaven's culture. These aren't just interesting ideas to think about. They're practical realities you can begin cultivating in your own life and community starting today.

Faith in the divine forms the foundation - not religious obligation but genuine trust in divine goodness and power that transforms how you see everything else. This isn't about trying harder to believe but about recognizing divine activity already happening in your life and letting that build your trust muscle over time.

Heavenly priorities rearrange what you value and chase after. Success gets redefined not by wealth accumulated or status achieved but by love expressed, people restored, and divine presence manifested. This shift in values changes how you use your time, money, talents, and influence in ways that often look foolish by worldly standards but produce a quality of life that material success can't deliver.

Divine revelation provides ongoing guidance beyond your own limited perspective. Through prayer, scripture, dreams, and spiritual promptings, you gain access to insights about yourself, others, and situations that you couldn't have figured out on your own. This partnership with divine wisdom leads to decisions and actions that often contradict conventional thinking but consistently produce better results.

Kingdom norms established the patterns of behavior that create environments where divine life flourishes naturally. Radical forgiveness, supernatural generosity, truthful speech, and joyful suffering become the new normal, not through rigid rule following but as natural expressions of a transformed heart.

So how do you move from understanding these components to actually experiencing them? Start by evaluating which component needs most development in your life right now. Is your trust in divine goodness shaky or inconsistent? Are you still chasing success as defined by your surrounding culture? Do you make decisions based solely on your own reasoning without seeking divine input? Have you adopted the behavioral norms of heaven's culture or are you still operating by the unwritten rules of earthly societies?

Next, identify one specific priority from your surrounding culture that contradicts heaven's values. Maybe it's the belief that your worth comes from your productivity. Or that financial security should be your primary goal. Or that looking good matters more than being real. Consciously challenge this assumption and experiment with living by the opposite value for thirty days. Notice what changes in your perspective and relationships.

Establish a daily practice for receiving divine revelation. This might be as simple as starting each morning with five minutes of silence, asking for guidance and then listening expectantly. Write down any impressions you receive, even if they seem insignificant. Over time, track which ones proved meaningful and learn to recognize the distinct quality of divine communication in your life.

Choose one kingdom norm to intentionally practice this week. If it's forgiveness, identify someone you've been resenting and take practical steps to release that burden. If it's generosity, find an opportunity to give in a way that stretches your comfort zone. If it's truthful speech, practice speaking with both accuracy and love in a situation where you'd normally hold back or exaggerate.

Finally, find others who want to cultivate these same components. Heaven's culture grows best in community, not in isolation. Create a small group where you can discuss your experiences, encourage each other's growth, and practice these realities together. Even two or three people committed to living this way can become a powerful outpost of heaven's culture in their larger community.

Remember that cultivating heaven's culture is a process, not an event. You won't perfect these components overnight. There will be steps forward and steps backward. The goal isn't flawless performance but genuine transformation that happens over time as you consistently align yourself with these divine realities.

The beautiful thing about heaven's culture is that it spreads naturally when lived authentically. You don't need to preach it or promote it.

People notice the difference in how you navigate life's challenges, make decisions, treat others, and maintain peace in difficult circumstances. Your life becomes a living invitation to experience a different reality than the one most people accept as normal.

As you integrate these four components - faith in the divine, heavenly priorities, divine revelation, and kingdom norms - you become a walking outpost of heaven's culture wherever you go. Your home, workplace, neighborhood, and relationships become spaces where divine reality breaks through in tangible ways. You become part of the quiet revolution that is secretly transforming earth right now, one life and one community at a time.

The world doesn't need more religious activity or even more human goodness. It needs people who embody heaven's culture in genuine, practical ways that address real problems and create authentic transformation. As you cultivate these four components in your daily life, you become exactly that kind of person - not through dramatic spiritual experiences or special religious knowledge, but through consistent alignment with the divine realities that have been transforming lives and communities since the beginning of time.

Heaven's culture isn't just coming someday in the future. It's available now, breaking into our world through ordinary people who have discovered these four components and chosen to live by them regardless of what their surrounding culture values or rewards. You can be one of those people starting today, creating a pocket of heaven's reality in your corner of the world that gradually expands to influence everything and everyone it touches.

The Cultural Battlefield: Systems vs. Symptoms

Beyond Individual Transformation

The secret plan of heaven goes deeper than most people think. It's not just about changing one heart at a time. While personal change matters, heaven has a bigger target in mind. It aims to transform entire systems - the hidden rules and patterns that shape how groups of people think and act together.

Think about water in a river. Each drop moves along, following the current. The drops don't create the current - the shape of the riverbed does. In the same way, many of our choices and problems don't come just from inside us. They come from the cultural "riverbeds" that guide how we live together.

These cultural systems work like invisible gravity fields pulling people toward certain behaviors. A workplace where gossip is normal makes it hard for even good people to speak well of others. A family with patterns of addiction creates powerful currents that pull new generations into the same struggles. A neighborhood where neighbors never talk builds walls of isolation that feel impossible to break through.

Heaven knows that helping one person swim against these currents helps that person but leaves the current unchanged. So while heaven cares deeply about individual hearts, its strategy targets the currents themselves. It works to reshape the cultural riverbeds so that the natural flow leads toward life instead of destruction.

This explains why some communities see sudden, widespread changes that can't be traced to any single person's efforts. The invisible systems shift, and everyone living in that cultural space begins to move differently without even knowing why. New patterns emerge that make harmful choices harder and life-giving choices easier.

I know a town that had been torn apart by racial tension for generations. Churches, schools, businesses - everything operated along deeply divided lines that everyone accepted as normal. Individual efforts to cross these boundaries usually failed. Then something shifted. No one can point to exactly when or how it started, but new connections formed. Unexpected friendships developed. Projects bringing different groups together succeeded where similar efforts had failed before. The cultural current itself had changed direction.

Heaven's infiltration strategy works at this deeper level, targeting not just what people do but the hidden agreements that make certain behaviors feel inevitable. It changes not just individual minds but shared assumptions that entire communities live by without questioning.

When you understand this system-level strategy, you start to see your personal transformation as part of something much bigger. Your changed heart becomes a beachhead for heaven's culture to spread into the systems around you. Your new patterns of thinking and acting create tiny cracks in cultural walls that once seemed impenetrable.

Identifying Cultural Strongholds

Every group of humans creates unwritten rules. These hidden agreements shape how people in that group think and act together. Most people follow these rules without ever noticing them. They feel as natural as gravity - just "the way things are."

These cultural agreements become strongholds when they lock people into harmful patterns that resist change. Like invisible fortresses, they protect destructive ways of living and make new possibilities seem impossible. They convince everyone inside them that "this is just how life works."

To spot these cultural strongholds, look for the unquestioned assumptions in any environment. Listen for phrases like "That's just how we do things here" or "That would never work in this community." These signal the presence of cultural agreements so deeply rooted that people can't imagine alternatives.

In many workplaces, a common stronghold is the belief that value comes from constant busyness. People race from meeting to meeting, answer emails at all hours, and wear exhaustion like a badge of honor. Anyone who sets healthy boundaries gets labeled as "not committed" or "not a team player." This unwritten rule creates burnout, damages families, and actually reduces real productivity - but questioning it feels almost impossible from inside the system.

Families develop their own cultural strongholds. Some operate by the unspoken rule that "we don't talk about painful things." Others enforce the belief that "showing weakness is dangerous." These agreements pass down through generations, shaping how people relate to each other in ways that block authentic connection and healing.

Communities hold shared assumptions too. Some neighborhoods silently agree that "you can't trust people who look different." Churches sometimes operate by the unwritten rule that "appearing spiritual matters more than being honest." Schools may enforce the belief that "certain kids just can't learn." These cultural agreements limit what people can imagine or attempt together.

To identify these strongholds in your own environments, pay attention to what feels "normal" but produces bad fruit. Notice which topics make people uncomfortable or defensive when questioned. Look for patterns that everyone complains about but no one seriously challenges. These point to the presence of cultural agreements that have hardened into strongholds.

Also watch for the "enforcers" - people who quickly correct anyone who violates the unwritten rules. They often use humor, shame, or appeals to tradition to pull others back into line. Their role in maintaining the cultural stronghold usually isn't conscious. They simply feel deeply uncomfortable when established patterns get disrupted.

The most powerful strongholds are those we've internalized so completely that we can't even see them. Like fish unaware of water, we swim in these cultural currents without noticing how they shape our thoughts and limit our choices. This is why an outside perspective becomes so valuable. People from different backgrounds can often spot the unwritten rules we've accepted as "just reality."

Heaven's infiltration strategy begins with making these invisible agreements visible. Once people can see the water they've been swimming in, they can begin to question whether these currents lead toward life or away from it. They can start to imagine alternatives that once seemed impossible.

I know a church that had operated for decades by the unwritten rule that "leadership means never showing weakness." Pastors burned out regularly but always in silence. When one leader finally named this cultural agreement and admitted his own struggles publicly, the stronghold began to crack. People could finally see the water they'd been swimming in. New possibilities for authentic leadership emerged that no one could have imagined before.

Identifying cultural strongholds isn't about finding someone to blame. These systems usually develop for understandable reasons and are maintained by good people with good intentions. The point isn't to attack the people inside these systems but to help everyone see the invisible walls that have been limiting what's possible.

The Domino Effect Strategy

Trying to change an entire cultural system at once rarely works. The system is too big, too complex, with too many interconnected parts all reinforcing each other. Frontal attacks on established cultures usually fail, creating only resistance and deeper entrenchment of the very patterns you hoped to change.

Heaven uses a smarter approach - the domino effect strategy. Instead of trying to transform everything at once, this approach identifies key leverage points where small changes can trigger cascading effects throughout the larger system.

Think about how domino's work. When set up in the right pattern, tipping just one small piece can eventually bring down structures thousands of times its size. The key is finding that first domino - the precise point where a small push will start a chain reaction.

In cultural systems, these leverage points often appear insignificant at first glance. They might be small rituals, seemingly minor language patterns, or relationships that don't look particularly important. Yet these points connect to other elements in ways that create ripple effects far beyond their apparent significance.

I know a company that transformed its toxic culture not through a major reorganization but by changing one simple meeting practice. They started every gathering by sharing recent successes, no matter how small. This tiny shift gradually changed how people talked to each other, how they viewed problems, what they noticed throughout the day, and ultimately how they worked together. One small domino tipped over led to massive changes throughout the system.

Heaven's infiltration strategy consistently targets these leverage points rather than attacking entire systems head-on. It looks for the smallest intervention that can create the largest effect. This approach requires patience and discernment to identify precisely where and how to apply pressure for maximum impact.

Sometimes the key leverage point is a specific relationship. One connection that bridges divided groups can eventually transform entire communities. I've seen neighborhoods change dramatically after just one family built authentic friendship with people from a different background. That single relationship became the first domino that eventually brought down walls of separation throughout the community.

Other times, the leverage point is a particular moment or event. A crisis that disrupts normal patterns. A celebration that brings diverse people together. A public acknowledgment of a painful truth that everyone knew but no one discussed. These moments create openings where new possibilities can enter systems that seemed permanently closed to change.

The domino effect strategy also looks for beliefs that function as linchpins holding other beliefs in place. In many cultural systems, a single core assumption supports numerous other ideas and practices. When that central belief shifts, everything built upon it becomes open to reconsideration.

For example, many religious communities operate on the unspoken belief that "God values religious performance." This single assumption creates endless activities designed to demonstrate spiritual commitment. When this core belief shifts to "God values authentic relationship," the entire system of religious behaviors suddenly comes into question. One domino affects everything else.

What makes this strategy so effective is that it requires minimal resources to initiate but generates maximum impact over time. Unlike approaches that demand overwhelming force or authority, the domino effect can begin with the actions of even one person with no official position or power.

This explains why heaven often works through unlikely people in seemingly small ways. The teenager whose simple question disrupts an unhealthy family pattern. The new employee whose fresh perspective reveals alternatives no one had considered. The quiet neighbor whose consistent kindness gradually thaws a cold community. These apparently minor influences can trigger chain reactions that transform entire cultural systems.

The domino effect strategy also explains why patience matters so much in cultural transformation. The full impact rarely appears immediately. The first domino falls, then the second, then the third - with the most significant changes often happening much later in the sequence. Those who demand instant, visible results usually give up before the most important dominoes begin to fall.

Creating Cultural Incubators

New cultures need safe spaces to develop. Just as babies grow in the protected environment of the womb before facing the outside world, heaven's culture needs incubators where its patterns can take root and strengthen before confronting entrenched opposing systems.

These cultural incubators are small, intentional communities that embody different ways of living together. They create working models that demonstrate the superiority of heaven's patterns over worldly systems. They don't just talk about alternative possibilities - they live them out in visible, tangible ways that others can observe and experience.

Unlike isolated communes that withdraw from society, effective cultural incubators maintain connection with the larger world. They create contrast without complete separation. They function as living laboratories where people can step in and out, experiencing the difference between heaven's culture and prevailing cultural systems.

I know a group of families who created such an incubator in a neighborhood known for isolation and fear. They began sharing meals together regularly and inviting others to join. They established patterns of sharing resources, watching each other's children, and helping with home repairs. They celebrated together and supported each other through crises. Over time, this small community became a visible demonstration of an alternative way of living that neighbors could observe firsthand.

What makes these incubators so powerful is that they don't just describe heaven's culture - they demonstrate it. They create spaces where people can taste and see the results of living by different rules. This experiential encounter proves far more convincing than any argument or explanation could be.

Effective cultural incubators share several key characteristics. First, they practice radical hospitality, welcoming outsiders without demanding conformity before inclusion. They create low thresholds for initial participation while maintaining clear identity and boundaries. This balance allows new people to experience the culture without diluting its distinctive qualities.

Second, these incubators explicitly name their values and practices. They don't just live differently - they help people understand why they make the choices they do. This naming process makes the invisible visible, helping participants recognize the cultural water they're swimming in rather than absorbing it unconsciously.

Third, successful incubators create regular rhythms and rituals that reinforce the alternative culture. Shared meals, celebration moments, conflict resolution practices, and other repeated experiences embed new patterns deeply into daily life. These rhythms gradually reshape how people think and relate, often without them even realizing the transformation happening.

Fourth, these communities maintain a learning posture rather than claiming to have perfected heaven's culture. They acknowledge their mistakes and limitations while continuing to pursue more authentic alignment with divine patterns. This humility makes them attractive in a world tired of religious arrogance and performance.

Cultural incubators serve as bridging environments between heaven's perfect culture and earth's broken systems. They don't achieve flawless implementation of divine patterns, but they create working models close enough to the original to demonstrate its superior results. They show what's possible when people begin living by different rules than those that govern surrounding cultures.

These incubators also provide safe spaces for people to detox from unhealthy cultural patterns they've absorbed. Many harmful ways of thinking and relating have become so normalized that people need time in an alternative environment to recognize and unlearn them. Cultural incubators offer that protected space for unlearning old patterns while practicing new ones.

Heaven's infiltration strategy uses these incubators as training grounds for agents who will eventually carry the alternative culture into other environments. People experience the contrast between heaven's patterns and worldly systems, internalize the difference, and then bring that new cultural DNA with them into workplaces, neighborhoods, schools, and other settings that desperately need transformation.

The most effective cultural incubators don't try to grow into massive institutions. They intentionally stay small enough to maintain authentic relationships while multiplying through new groups rather than endless expansion. Like healthy cells dividing, they reproduce their cultural DNA through new communities that carry the same essential patterns while adapting to different contexts.

Recap: Engaging the Cultural Battlefield

You've now discovered how heaven's strategy targets entire cultural systems, not just individual hearts and behaviors. This bigger-picture approach explains why some transformation efforts produce lasting change while others create only temporary improvements that quickly fade.

You've learned to identify cultural strongholds - those unwritten rules and shared assumptions that shape communities and perpetuate patterns of brokenness. These invisible agreements often have more power than official policies or individual choices in determining what happens in families, workplaces, neighborhoods, and other social environments.

You've explored the domino effect strategy that heaven uses to transform systems that seem too entrenched to change. By identifying key leverage points - specific relationships, moments, or beliefs that connect to many other elements - this approach creates cascading effects that eventually transform entire cultures through relatively small initial interventions.

You've seen how cultural incubators serve as living laboratories where heaven's alternative patterns can take root and demonstrate their superior results. These intentional communities don't just talk about different ways of living - they embody them in visible, tangible forms that others can experience directly.

Now it's time to apply these insights to your own cultural environments. Start by mapping the unwritten rules operating in one setting you regularly inhabit - perhaps your workplace, family, church, or neighborhood. What behaviors get rewarded in this environment? What actions or questions make people uncomfortable? What assumptions does everyone take for granted without examination?

Look for the pain points in this cultural system. Where do people consistently struggle? What problems keep recurring despite attempts to address them? Which solutions have been tried but failed? These trouble spots often reveal the presence of cultural strongholds that need transformation rather than just individual behavior changes.

Next, identify potential leverage points where small changes might create ripple effects throughout this system. Is there a key relationship that could bridge divided groups? A specific practice that reinforces unhealthy patterns? A core belief that supports numerous other assumptions? These points offer opportunities for strategic intervention with maximum impact.

Consider what alternative pattern you could begin practicing that would challenge a cultural assumption in this environment. Not as a frontal attack that provokes resistance, but as a quiet demonstration of a different possibility. Perhaps consistently speaking well of others in a gossip-prone workplace. Or asking genuine questions in a family that avoids real conversation. Or connecting divided neighbors through simple hospitality in a fragmented community.

Finally, look for others who sense the same need for cultural transformation. You don't need many people to create an effective incubator - even two or three committed individuals can establish patterns that eventually influence much larger systems. Start practicing heaven's alternative culture together in ways visible enough for others to notice but humble enough to avoid triggering defensive reactions.

Remember that cultural transformation happens on a different timeline than individual change. Systems shift slowly at first, with much of the initial change happening below the surface where it's hard to see. Be patient and persistent, knowing that the most significant breakthroughs often come after long periods where nothing seems to be happening.

As you engage this cultural battlefield, maintain the paradoxical balance that characterizes heaven's approach. Be bold in vision but humble in method. Hold firmly to divine values while adapting flexibly to each specific context. Challenge broken systems while loving the people caught in them. This balanced approach avoids both passive acceptance of destructive patterns and aggressive confrontation that only hardens resistance.

The cultural battlefield may seem overwhelming at times. Entrenched systems have massive momentum and powerful defenders. But heaven's infiltration strategy has been overcoming such obstacles since the beginning of time. It doesn't depend on human resources, credentials, or platforms. It works through ordinary people who recognize cultural strongholds, identify strategic leverage points, and create living demonstrations of a better way.

You are now equipped to be one of those people - not because you have special abilities or authority, but because you understand how cultural systems work and how heaven's strategy transforms them. Your changed perspective makes you dangerous to strongholds that have survived countless frontal attacks but remain vulnerable to the quiet, persistent influence of heaven's culture embodied through ordinary people in everyday settings.

The invasion of heaven's culture happens not just through dramatic spiritual experiences but through the patient, strategic reshaping of cultural systems that guide how communities think and live together. As you participate in this deeper transformation, you become part of a divine strategy that isn't just changing individual lives but creating entire environments where heaven's patterns become the new normal.

The Resistance Response: What Happens

When Systems Fight Back

Recognizing Systemic Pushback

When heaven's culture starts to spread, something predictable happens. The systems it challenges don't just sit back and watch. They fight back. This pushback isn't random or accidental. It's a natural response when an established system feels threatened.

Think about what happens when your body detects a foreign substance. Your immune system activates, sending white blood cells to attack the invader and protect your body's normal functioning. Systems of darkness work the same way. When they detect heaven's culture infiltrating their territory, they launch protective responses designed to eliminate the threat and restore their version of "normal."

This resistance often starts subtly. You might notice increased pressure to conform to the old patterns. A workplace that never cared about punctuality suddenly becomes strict about start times when you begin building authentic relationships there. A family system comfortable with its dysfunction finds reasons why your healthier boundaries are "selfish" or "uncaring." A religious community that tolerated your questions starts labeling them as dangerous or divisive when those questions threaten established power structures.

The pushback usually intensifies as heaven's influence grows. What began as gentle pressure became active opposition. The obstacles multiply. The criticism gets louder. The isolation increases. This progression isn't a sign that something's wrong with your approach. It's evidence that the infiltration is working. The system wouldn't bother fighting back if your presence wasn't making a real difference.

I know a teacher who began bringing heaven's compassion into a school with a rigid, performance-focused culture. At first, her different approach drew little attention. But when students in her classroom started thriving in ways that highlighted problems in the wider system, the pushback began. Suddenly her teaching methods faced unusual scrutiny. Her requests for resources met mysterious delays. Colleagues who initially seemed supportive grew distant. The system was defending itself against the alternative culture she represented.

This resistance shows up in predictable forms. First comes the pressure to compromise "just a little" on the values that made the difference in the first place. Then come unexpected obstacles that make continuing the new patterns difficult or costly. Relationships often complicate as people who seem supportive reveal their deeper loyalty to the existing system. Internal doubts arise, making you question whether the opposition means you've somehow misunderstood your assignment.

Recognizing this pushback for what it is—a systemic immune response rather than a personal attack—changes how you experience it. Instead of being surprised or discouraged when resistance appears, you can see it as confirmation that your presence is having a real impact. The stronger the pushback, the clearer the evidence that heaven's culture is successfully infiltrating territory previously controlled by opposing systems.

This perspective transforms opposition from something to fear into something to anticipate as a normal part of the infiltration process. Just as a doctor expects a fever when the body fights infection, you can expect systemic resistance when heaven's culture begins displacing established patterns of darkness. The resistance doesn't mean you're doing something wrong. It means the medicine is working.

The Unexpected Opposition

When you first step into your role as a carrier of heaven's culture, you might expect opposition from obvious sources. The openly hostile. The deliberately destructive. They are clearly opposed to everything good and right. But these aren't usually the ones who create the strongest resistance.

The most effective opposition often comes from places and people you never anticipated. Religious systems frequently generate the fiercest pushback against genuine divine activity. People who use spiritual language and claim to represent God's interests become surprisingly uncomfortable when heaven's culture appears in forms they don't control or understand.

This pattern isn't new. Throughout history, the strongest opposition to divine breakthroughs has consistently come from religious institutions and leaders who felt threatened by expressions of spiritual reality outside their approved structures. Their resistance feels especially confusing and painful because it comes wrapped in spiritual language and justified by appeals to tradition, scripture, or protection of the community.

I know a young woman who began experiencing remarkable spiritual insights that brought healing to people around her. She wasn't trying to start a movement or challenge any authority. She simply responded to what heaven showed her. The strongest opposition came not from secular sources but from religious leaders who questioned her credentials, demanded she submit to their oversight, and eventually labeled her experiences as dangerous when she couldn't fit them into existing religious categories.

Even more surprising is the resistance that comes from friends and family who initially supported your journey. These relationships often shift when your transformation starts creating uncomfortable contrasts. Your growing freedom highlights their continued bondage. Your new perspectives challenge their unquestioned assumptions. Your changing priorities make them feel judged even when you've said nothing critical about their choices.

This relational resistance hurts more than opposition from strangers or systems because it feels like betrayal. The people you expected to cheer you on become cautious, critical, or distant. They might express concern about how you're changing or suggest you're becoming "too extreme." They may try to pull you back to your former self through guilt, nostalgia, or appeals to loyalty.

But perhaps the most unexpected source of opposition comes from within yourself. Parts of your own thinking and identity have been shaped by the very systems heaven's culture is now challenging. These internal patterns don't surrender easily. They fight for survival, generating doubts, fears, and rationalizations for returning to familiar territory even when you consciously want to move forward.

This inner resistance often speaks in your own voice, making it particularly difficult to recognize. It disguises itself as wisdom, caution, or common sense. "Maybe I'm taking this too far." "What if I'm misunderstanding what God wants?" "Is this really worth the conflict it's creating?" These thoughts don't come from divine guidance but from internal programming designed to maintain the status quo.

Understanding these unexpected sources of opposition helps you prepare for them without becoming paranoid or defensive. You can anticipate that religious systems may feel threatened by authentic divine activity outside their control. You can expect that some relationships will struggle to adjust to your transformation. You can recognize that parts of your own thinking will resist the very changes you consciously desire.

This awareness doesn't make the opposition less painful, but it does make it less confusing. Instead of being blindsided by resistance from sources you thought would support heaven's work, you can see these reactions as normal parts of the infiltration process. Systems fight to preserve themselves—whether those systems exist in religious institutions, family dynamics, or your own established patterns of thinking.

The unexpected nature of this opposition actually serves a divine purpose. It reveals the true extent of darkness's influence in places we assumed were already aligned with heaven. It exposes how thoroughly worldly values have infiltrated even religious spaces and relationships. And it shows how deeply we've internalized systemic patterns that contradict heaven's culture. This painful clarity, while difficult to face, creates opportunity for more complete transformation.

Weaponized Discouragement

When systems of darkness fight back against heaven's infiltration, they deploy many weapons. But their most effective strategy isn't physical opposition or even direct confrontation. It's weaponized discouragement—a sophisticated attack that targets your emotional resilience and spiritual stamina.

This strategy works because it's indirect. Instead of opposing your activities directly, it drains your motivation to continue them. Instead of arguing against your message, it makes you question whether sharing it matters. Instead of blocking your path, it makes the journey feel too exhausting to complete.

Weaponized discouragement follows predictable patterns. First comes isolation—the subtle separation from supportive relationships that might strengthen your resolve. This happens through scheduling conflicts, communication barriers, misunderstandings, or simply the busyness that makes maintaining connection difficult. The system works to ensure you face opposition alone, without the encouragement and perspective that community provides.

Next comes confusion about God's voice. The very clarity you once had about your assignment gets clouded with doubts and conflicting messages. You find yourself uncertain whether you heard correctly or if you've somehow misunderstood. This confusion rarely comes as direct contradiction. Instead, it arrives as plausible alternatives, reasonable questions, and spiritual-sounding concerns that create just enough uncertainty to stall your momentum.

Then the consequences get exaggerated. Small setbacks are magnified to look like complete failure. Temporary resistance appears as permanent rejection. Limited opposition feels like universal condemnation. This distortion makes continuing seem pointless—why keep going when everything indicates you're making no progress or even causing harm?

Finally comes the most devastating lie: nothing is changing. Despite evidence that your presence is making a difference, you're fed the perception that your efforts are wasted. The system highlights every sign of continued darkness while hiding the growing light. It points to persistent problems while concealing emerging solutions. It keeps your attention on what hasn't changed rather than what has.

I know a man who began bringing heaven's culture into a community marked by racial division. He built relationships across boundaries that had separated people for generations. But as his work gained traction, weaponized discouragement attacked from all sides. Former friends withdrew, leaving him feeling isolated. spiritual leaders raised questions about his methods, creating confusion about whether he was truly following divine guidance. Every setback received enormous attention while breakthroughs were minimized. After months of this pressure, he nearly abandoned the work—not because of direct opposition but because discouragement had drained his hope that change was possible.

This weapon proves especially effective against those with genuine humility and sensitivity. People who care deeply about doing the right thing become vulnerable to suggestions that they're causing harm. Those who value community feel the pain of isolation more acutely. Thoughtful individuals take seriously the possibility they might be mistaken. These admirable qualities become entry points for weaponized discouragement.

The strategic deployment of discouragement reveals how seriously darkness takes heaven's infiltration. Systems don't waste resources defending against minor threats. They reserve their most sophisticated weapons for genuine dangers to their control. When you face this kind of weaponized discouragement, it's perverse confirmation of your effectiveness. The opposition wouldn't invest so heavily in discouraging you if your presence wasn't making a real difference.

Recognizing this strategy for what it is provides your first defense against it. When you understand that the discouragement itself is a weapon rather than a reality, you can begin to question its messages. Is the isolation as complete as it feels, or are supportive relationships still available? Is divine guidance really as unclear as it seems, or has confusion been artificially introduced? Are the setbacks as significant as they appear, or have they been magnified? Is nothing truly changing, or has attention been diverted from real progress?

This recognition doesn't instantly remove the feelings of discouragement, but it does create space to question their validity and resist their purpose. The weapon's power diminishes significantly once you identify it as a strategic attack rather than an accurate reflection of reality.

Supernatural Resilience Strategies

Heaven doesn't send its agents into battle without protection. For every weapon formed against its infiltration, divine wisdom provides specific counter-strategies. These aren't complicated techniques requiring special training. They're practical approaches anyone can implement to maintain momentum when facing systemic resistance.

The first strategy involves perspective shifts that transform how you see opposition. When resistance intensifies, heaven provides the ability to reinterpret what's happening from a divine viewpoint. What looks like failure from ground level appears as strategic progress when seen from above. What feels like rejection becomes protection from premature alliances. What seems like an ending reveals itself as a necessary transition to the next phase.

These perspective shifts aren't positive thinking or denial of difficulties. They're accurate recognitions of what's really happening beneath surface appearances. Like soldiers who understand the larger battle strategy, heaven's agents can endure current challenges because they see how these fit into the broader campaign. This divine viewpoint doesn't eliminate the pain of opposition but places it within a meaningful context that makes it bearable.

I know a woman whose efforts to bring reconciliation to a divided church seemed to explode in her face. Leaders rejected her approaches. Relationships fractured further. The situation appeared worse than before she started. In her discouragement, she received a dream showing how the current "failure" was actually exposing hidden issues that had to be revealed before genuine healing could begin. This perspective shift didn't make the situation less painful, but it transformed her understanding of what was happening and renewed her hope.

The second resilience strategy involves strategic rest—not as escape from difficulty but as preparation for sustained effectiveness. Unlike worldly systems that value constant activity and measure commitment by exhaustion, heaven's culture includes rhythms of withdrawal and renewal. These aren't signs of weakness but essential elements of supernatural resilience.

This strategic rest looks different from mere recreation or distraction. It involves intentional disengagement from the battlefield to reconnect with divine presence, regain spiritual perspective, and allow deep renewal of depleted resources. It might include physical withdrawal to quiet places, immersion in beauty that reminds you what you're fighting for, or engagement with scripture and prayer that reorients your thinking to divine reality.

The timing of this rest often proves as important as the rest itself. Heaven's wisdom knows precisely when withdrawal serves the mission better than continued engagement. Learning to recognize these moments—when pressing forward would deplete you beyond recovery but strategic rest will prepare you for greater effectiveness—becomes a crucial skill for sustainable impact.

The third resilience strategy involves community reinforcement. Heaven rarely sends its agents into difficult territories alone. It surrounds them with strategic relationships that provide perspective, encouragement, and practical support during periods of intense opposition. These connections create resilience far beyond what any individual could maintain in isolation.

These reinforcing relationships don't always look like formal support teams. They might include friends who know nothing about your specific assignment but provide emotional refreshment when you're depleted. They might be mentors who've walked similar paths and can normalize what you're experiencing. They might even be people you know only through their writings or teachings but whose perspectives help you interpret your experiences accurately.

The fourth and perhaps most counterintuitive resilience strategy involves celebrating opposition as confirmation. Heaven's agents learn to recognize resistance as evidence they're making genuine impact. The absence of pushback often indicates ineffectiveness, while intensifying opposition suggests you're disrupting systems in meaningful ways. This recognition transforms discouragement into strange encouragement— the resistance itself becomes proof you're on the right track.

This celebration doesn't mean enjoying suffering or seeking opposition unnecessarily. It simply acknowledges the predictable response when light enters darkness. Systems don't bother fighting what poses no threat to their control. The strength of the resistance often correlates directly with the significance of the breakthrough you represent.

These supernatural resilience strategies work together to create sustainability that confounds opposing systems. When heaven's agents should be depleted by resistance, they find themselves renewed. When they should be discouraged by setbacks, they discover fresh hope. When they should abandon their assignments due to opposition, they develop deeper commitment. This unexplainable resilience itself becomes evidence of divine support that no human resources could provide.

Unlike worldly endurance based on willpower and determination, supernatural resilience flows from connection with divine resources that never deplete. It doesn't deny the reality of opposition or minimize its difficulty. It simply ensures that heaven's agents can continue their assignments despite resistance that would stop anyone relying solely on human strength.

Recap: Thriving Through Resistance

You've now discovered why opposition intensifies when heaven's culture successfully infiltrates established systems. This resistance isn't random or accidental—it's a predictable immune response when darkness detects a genuine threat to its control. Understanding this pattern transforms how you experience pushback, helping you see it as confirmation of effectiveness rather than evidence of failure.

You've learned about the unexpected sources of opposition that often create the strongest resistance. Religious systems frequently fight hardest against authentic divine activity they don't control. Friends and family sometimes pull back when your transformation creates uncomfortable contrasts with their choices. Even your own internal programming may generate resistance to the very changes you consciously desire. Recognizing these sources helps you respond to them without confusion or paranoia.

You've explored how systems weaponize discouragement to drain your motivation when they can't directly stop your activities. Through isolation, confusion about divine guidance, exaggeration of setbacks, and the lie that nothing is changing, this sophisticated strategy targets your emotional and spiritual stamina. Identifying this weapon for what it is provides your first defense against its effectiveness.

You've discovered supernatural resilience strategies that enable continued effectiveness despite opposition. Divine perspective shifts transform how you interpret resistance. Strategic rest prepares you for sustained impact. Community reinforcement provides support when isolation threatens. Celebrating opposition as confirmation turns discouragement into validation. These approaches create sustainability beyond what human resources alone could maintain.

So how do you apply these insights to your current situation? Start by identifying which form of resistance you're experiencing right now. Is it increasing pressure to conform to old patterns? Unexpected obstacles to continued progress? Relationship complications with people who initially supported you? Internal doubts about whether you've understood your assignment correctly? Naming the specific form of opposition helps you respond appropriately rather than reacting to all resistance in the same way.

Next, examine whether you're experiencing weaponized discouragement. Do you feel unusually isolated from supportive relationships? Has your clarity about divine guidance become clouded with confusion? Are setbacks being magnified to look like complete failure? Does it seem like nothing is changing despite evidence to the contrary? Recognizing these patterns as strategic attacks rather than accurate reflections of reality diminishes their power over your emotions and decisions.

Connect with others who can provide perspective during periods of intense opposition. This doesn't require finding people who understand every aspect of your assignment. Sometimes the most helpful perspectives come from those who simply know you well enough to remind you of your core identity and calling when circumstances make these hard to remember. Their outside viewpoint can help you distinguish between accurate discernment and weaponized discouragement.

Establish regular practices that renew your spiritual resilience before opposition intensifies. Don't wait until you're depleted to implement strategic rest. Create rhythms that consistently reconnect you with divine presence, realign your thinking with heaven's perspective, and replenish your emotional resources. These practices aren't luxuries for easy seasons—they're essential preparation for inevitable resistance.

Learn to recognize discouragement as a strategic attack rather than a spiritual reality. When waves of hopelessness, futility, or doubt wash over you, pause to question their source and purpose. Ask whether these feelings align with what you know about divine character and promises. Consider whether they serve heaven's purposes or opposing agendas. This questioning doesn't instantly remove the feelings, but it does create space to choose your response rather than being controlled by emotional weather.

Perhaps most importantly, celebrate resistance as confirmation you're making a genuine impact. When opposition intensifies, resist the natural interpretation that something has gone wrong. Consider the alternative explanation—things are going right, and systems of darkness are responding to a legitimate threat to their control. This perspective transforms discouragement into strange encouragement, helping you persist precisely when opposition wants you to quit.

Remember that periods of intense resistance often directly precede significant breakthroughs. Systems fight hardest when their control is most threatened. The darkest hour comes just before dawn. This pattern appears repeatedly throughout history—the most severe opposition arising right before transformative change manifests. Recognizing this timing can help you maintain hope and momentum through the most difficult phases of resistance.

The resistance response you're experiencing isn't evidence that heaven's infiltration strategy has failed. It's confirmation that the strategy is working exactly as intended. Systems don't fight what poses no threat. They don't waste resources opposing ineffective intrusions. The very fact that you're facing increasing pushback suggests you're carrying something genuine that darkness recognizes as dangerous to its continued control.

As you implement these approaches for thriving through resistance, you'll discover a paradoxical truth: opposition often accelerates the very transformation it intends to prevent. The system's immune response, meant to eliminate heaven's influence, frequently exposes weaknesses and contradictions that make the need for change more obvious. What darkness intends as a weapon against infiltration becomes a catalyst that hastens its own displacement.

This understanding doesn't make resistance painless or simple to navigate. The opposition remains real and often intensely difficult. But seeing it within the larger context of heaven's infiltration strategy transforms how you experience and respond to it. Instead of being surprised, confused, or discouraged by resistance, you recognize it as a normal and even necessary part of the process through which heaven's culture gradually displaces systems of darkness on earth.

The Tipping Point: When Heaven's Culture Breaks Through

The Breakthrough Pattern

Have you ever planted seeds in a garden? You put them in the soil, water them, and wait. For days or even weeks, nothing seems to happen. The ground looks exactly the same as when you started. Then suddenly, almost overnight, tiny green shoots appear. What looked like nothing was actually intense activity happening underground, invisible to your eyes.

Heaven's work follows this same pattern. Long periods of apparent inactivity suddenly give way to a visible breakthrough. This isn't random or unpredictable - it's a consistent pattern that plays out in homes, workplaces, neighborhoods, and entire cities. Understanding this pattern helps you make sense of those frustrating seasons when nothing seems to be changing despite your faithful efforts.

The breakthrough pattern has three distinct phases. First comes the underground phase, where heaven's culture spreads beneath the surface through changed hearts, quiet conversations, small acts of kindness, and shifts in individual thinking. Nothing looks different on the outside. The systems still operate as they always have. Harmful patterns continue unchallenged. To most observers, nothing significant is happening.

During this underground phase, heaven's agents often struggle with discouragement. They see little evidence that their efforts matter.

They wonder if they've misunderstood their assignment or if they're doing something wrong. The lack of visible results tests their trust and patience. Many give up just before breakthrough would have appeared, not realizing how much has been happening beneath the surface.

The second phase begins with small visible changes - tiny cracks in previously solid systems. A leader unexpectedly supports an idea they would have rejected before. A long-standing conflict suddenly finds resolution. A person known for resistance shows surprising openness. These small shifts might seem random or insignificant when viewed individually. But together, they signal that the underground work has reached a critical mass.

I know a school where teachers had been praying for years with no apparent change in the toxic culture. Then small things started happening. A principal known for harsh criticism began asking for input. Two departments that had always competed began collaborating. Parents who had been hostile became supportive. Each change seemed minor, but together they revealed that something significant was shifting beneath the surface.

The final phase is a visible breakthrough, when transformation becomes undeniable. Systems that seemed permanently broken suddenly function in new ways. Relationships that appeared hopelessly damaged find healing. Resources that were always lacking suddenly became available. Obstacles that blocked progress for years disappear almost overnight. The change happens so quickly and completely that even skeptics struggle to explain it through normal causes.

What makes this pattern confusing is the timing. The underground phase often lasts much longer than we expect - sometimes years or even decades. Then the visible advancements happens much faster than seems possible, sometimes in days or weeks. This uneven timing creates the illusion that nothing was happening and then everything suddenly changed. In reality, the breakthrough was being prepared all along through invisible processes working beneath the surface.

Understanding this pattern prevents premature discouragement during long underground seasons. When you know that invisible work precedes visible change, you can maintain hope and momentum even when nothing seems to be happening. You recognize that lack of visible results doesn't mean lack of progress. The seeds are germinating underground, preparing for a breakthrough that will appear suddenly when the time is right.

Signs of Imminent Breakthroughs

While the timing of advancements often surprises us, it rarely happens without warning. Specific indicators signal when a tipping point approaches. Learning to recognize these signs helps you prepare for the sudden shift from underground work to visible transformation.

The first and most counterintuitive sign is increased resistance. When systems sense they're losing control, they fight back harder. Opposition intensifies. Criticism gets louder. Obstacles multiply. Many people misinterpret this escalating resistance as evidence that things are getting worse. In reality, it often signals that breakthrough is imminent. The systems wouldn't waste energy fighting something that posed no threat to their continued dominance.

Think about what happens just before a dam breaks. The pressure against the wall increases dramatically. The structure strains and creaks. Signs of stress appear throughout the system. These aren't indications that the dam is holding firm - they're warnings that collapse is approaching. In the same way, intensified opposition often directly precedes breakthrough as systems make their final, desperate attempt to maintain control.

The second sign involves unusual unity among kingdom agents. People who have been working separately suddenly find themselves drawn together. Connections form across boundaries that previously divided them. Different approaches and emphases that seemed contradictory start to complement each other. This supernatural coordination happens without human planning, as though an invisible hand is moving diverse pieces into position for a coordinated breakthrough.

I witnessed this in a city where various ministries and community organizations had operated independently for years. Each focused on their specific area - homelessness, education, addiction recovery, business development. Then, without any central organizing effort, leaders from these different groups began connecting. They discovered their work fit together like puzzle pieces forming a complete picture. This unexpected unity preceded a city-wide transformation that none could have accomplished alone.

The third indicator involves prophetic dreams and visions. As breakthrough approaches, people begin receiving similar messages through different channels. Someone has a dream showing transformation in their workplace. Another person gets a mental picture during prayer that portrays the same theme. Someone else finds their thoughts repeatedly drawn to a specific scripture that speaks of restoration.

These separate experiences contain common elements that confirm something significant is approaching.

These prophetic experiences often include specific details about how the breakthrough will unfold. They might reveal which relationships will be key, which obstacles will disappear, or which resources will suddenly become available. They frequently portray the transformation in symbolic language that becomes clear only as events unfold. Paying attention to these prophetic signals provides strategic advantage for cooperating with the approaching advancements.

The fourth sign involves strategic relationships forming across previous boundaries. People who would normally never connect suddenly find themselves in conversation. The business leader meets the community organizer. The artist connects with the engineer. The young activist finds common ground with the traditional religious leader. These unexpected relationships create bridges across divided territories, establishing pathways for heaven's culture to flow into previously isolated areas.

What makes these connections significant is their timing and specificity. They aren't random networking but precisely targeted relationships that create exactly the connections needed for the approaching breakthrough. Each brings together complementary gifts, perspectives, or resources that will prove essential when transformation accelerates.

Another indicator involves what we might call "atmosphere shifts" - subtle changes in the spiritual climate that sensitive people detect before visible transformation appears. The heaviness that characterized a place for years suddenly feels lighter. Conversations that always turned negative begin including hope. Creative solutions emerge where only problems were discussed before. These atmospheric shifts often feel fragile and inconsistent at first, strengthening as breakthrough approaches.

One of the most reliable signs involves unusual favor with gatekeepers. People who control access to resources, opportunities, or influence unexpectedly support heaven's agenda. The bank approved the loan that seemed impossible. The government official grants the permit that was repeatedly denied. The property owner offers space at a fraction of market rate. These instances of favor often make no sense from a natural perspective but create essential pathways for advancements to spread when it arrives.

Recognizing these indicators serves several important purposes. It confirms that your underground work hasn't been wasted, even when visible results remain minimal. It helps you prepare practically for the acceleration that comes with advancementss. Most importantly, it positions you to cooperate strategically with the approaching transformation rather than being surprised when long-established patterns suddenly shift.

Stewarding the Advancements

When advancements finally arrives after long seasons of underground work, many people make a crucial mistake. They assume the hardest part is over. In reality, stewarding advancements requires as much wisdom and diligence as preparing for it. Without proper stewardship, even dramatic transformations can fade quickly, leaving people more discouraged than before.

The first principle of stewarding advancements involves protecting it from premature publicity. When visible transformation begins, the natural impulse is to broadcast it widely. We want to celebrate publicly, share testimonies broadly, and let everyone know what God has done. While celebration matters, premature exposure often damages fragile advancements before they fully establish.

Like a premature baby needs protection from elements that wouldn't harm a fullterm infant, new breakthroughs need sheltering from forces that could overwhelm them. Media attention often distorts the essence of what's happening. Outside experts try to analyze and categorize the transformation according to existing frameworks. Well-meaning visitors want to observe and replicate the results without understanding the process that produced them. These pressures can easily derail genuine transformation before it fully matures.

I've seen promising community renewals collapse under the weight of publicity. What began as authentic transformation became a performance for outside observers. The focus shifted from the work itself to managing perceptions about the work. The genuine became contrived as people tried to maintain an image of success. Eventually, divine life drained away, leaving only empty forms that mimicked the original breakthrough.

The second principle involves resisting the urge to institutionalize too quickly. When breakthroughs create something beautiful, we naturally want to preserve and protect it. We create structures, establish leadership hierarchies, codify practices, and develop systems to maintain what we've experienced. While some organization eventually becomes necessary, premature institutionalization often kills the heavenly life it intends to protect.

Breakthrough moments thrive on flexibility, responsiveness, and direct divine guidance. They operate according to organic principles rather than mechanical ones. Trying to capture this organic life in rigid structures too quickly is like pressing a butterfly into a book to preserve its beauty. You may maintain the form, but you lose the living essence that made it beautiful in the first place.

The third principle for stewarding breakthrough involves maintaining the conditions that produced it. Transformations don't happen randomly. They emerge from specific spiritual and relational environments that heaven has carefully cultivated. When breakthrough comes, people often abandon the very practices that created space for divine activity, assuming they're no longer necessary now that results have appeared.

The prayer gatherings that preceded breakthrough get neglected because "we're too busy implementing the vision." The humble dependence on divine guidance gets replaced by confident strategic planning. The authentic relationships that formed the foundation for transformation take a back seat to programs and activities. As these foundational elements erode, the breakthrough gradually loses its supernatural quality and becomes just another human project.

Another crucial aspect of stewarding breakthrough involves recognizing and resisting counter-movements. When heaven's culture visibly breaks through, opposing systems don't simply surrender. They launch sophisticated counter-attacks designed to neutralize the transformation or redirect it toward lesser goals. These responses come in predictable forms that wise stewards learn to recognize and address.

One common counter-movement involves dilution - accepting the language and some external forms of the breakthrough while emptying it of transformative power. Religious systems excel at this strategy, absorbing new movements by adopting their terminology and some practices while subtly redirecting their core energy away from genuine transformation. What began as revolutionary becomes merely a variation on existing patterns.

Another counter-strategy involves division - creating conflicts among those experiencing the breakthrough by highlighting differences in approach, emphasis, or understanding. These conflicts drain energy from the transformation itself, redirecting focus to internal disputes rather than continued breakthrough. Before long, what began as a unified movement fragments into competing factions, each claiming to represent the "true" expression of the original breakthrough.

Perhaps the most subtle counter-movement involves distraction - shifting attention from the core transformation to secondary issues or opportunities. New doors open. Exciting possibilities appear. What seems like expansion actually disperses energy and focus that should remain concentrated until the breakthrough fully establishes. The transformation doesn't get directly opposed but simply diluted through diversification beyond sustainable limits.

Effective stewardship requires discernment to distinguish between genuine growth and these counter-movements. It involves maintaining focus on the essential core of the breakthrough rather than being pulled toward every opportunity that appears. It requires courage to protect the integrity of the transformation even when doing so appears unnecessarily restrictive to outside observers.

The ultimate goal of stewarding breakthroughs isn't preservation but multiplication. Heaven's strategy doesn't aim for isolated pockets of transformation but for breakthrough that spreads until entire cultures shift. Wise stewards balance protecting the integrity of what's happened with creating pathways for it to expand beyond its original boundaries.

From Infiltration to Occupation

Breakthrough moments, however powerful, are not the final goal of heaven's strategy. They're important milestones in a longer process that moves from initial infiltration through visible breakthrough to complete cultural occupation. Understanding this progression helps maintain proper perspective when breakthrough finally comes.

Infiltration represents the first phase, where heaven's agents quietly establish presence in territories dominated by opposing systems. This underground work creates networks, builds relationships, demonstrates alternative patterns, and prepares the ground for visible change. Though largely invisible to casual observers, this phase lays essential foundations without which breakthrough cannot last.

Breakthrough marks the tipping point where heaven's culture becomes visibly dominant in specific areas. Systems that resisted change suddenly transform. Relationships that seemed permanently broken find healing. Resources that were always lacking become abundantly available. These dramatic shifts provide undeniable evidence that something supernatural has happened.

Occupation represents the final phase, where heaven's culture becomes the new normal. Divine patterns no longer appear exceptional or temporary but establish themselves as the default way of operating. What began as isolated outposts of transformation spread until they connected, creating unified territories where heaven's culture predominates.

This occupation doesn't happen through force or control. It spreads through demonstrated superiority that makes previous ways of living obsolete. Like electric light replacing oil lamps, heaven's culture doesn't need to attack darkness directly - it simply provides such a clearly better alternative that old patterns lose their appeal and gradually disappear.

I've watched this progression in specific communities where heaven's infiltration strategy has advanced further than most places. What began with a few isolated individuals living by different values gradually reached a breakthrough, creating visible transformation that surprised even longtime residents. Now, years later, heaven's patterns have become so established that new people moving into these communities naturally adopt them without questioning. Divine culture has moved from infiltration through breakthrough to occupation.

The transition from breakthrough to occupation involves several key developments. First, the supernatural becomes natural - practices that once seemed extraordinary become normal parts of daily life. People expect divine guidance, provision, and intervention rather than being surprised by them. The miraculous doesn't disappear but becomes integrated into ordinary experience rather than standing apart from it.

Second, training replaces convincing - energy shifts from proving that heaven's culture works to equipping people to participate in what's already visibly successful. The question changes from "Is this real?" to "How can I be part of it?" This shift creates rapidly expanding capacity as resources previously spent overcoming skepticism get redirected toward developing new participants.

Third, systems align with values - organizational structures, economic models, educational approaches, and governance methods gradually transform to embody heaven's culture rather than merely accommodating it. What began as countercultural outposts eventually reshaped the surrounding systems until the entire infrastructure supported divine patterns.

Perhaps most significantly, the children born into these environments know nothing else. Unlike their parents who had to unlearn worldly patterns before embracing heaven's culture, these next-generation carriers inherit divine perspectives as their native mindset. They advance the occupation not through conscious effort but simply by living naturally from what they've always known.

This progression from infiltration through breakthrough to occupation rarely happens smoothly or completely in this lifetime. Most territories experience a mixed reality where heaven's culture has broken through in some areas while infiltration continues in others. Some aspects of community life reflect divine patterns while others remain under opposing influence. The occupation advances unevenly, creating a patchwork of transformation rather than uniform change.

Understanding this uneven progress prevents both premature celebration and unnecessary discouragement. We neither claim complete victory before it's achieved nor despair when significant territories remain under opposing control. We recognize that occupation advances through persistent presence and demonstrated superiority rather than dramatic conquest.

The ultimate goal remains complete transformation where divine patterns become so established that alternatives no longer appeal or even make sense. Like societies that once accepted slavery but now find it unthinkable, territories fully occupied by heaven's culture eventually lose even the memory of how things operated under previous systems.

This complete occupation rarely happens quickly. It advances through generations rather than months or years. The full manifestation may not appear within our lifetime. But understanding the progression helps us recognize our specific assignment within the larger strategy. Some are called to initial infiltration, others to stewarding breakthrough moments, and still others to establishing longterm occupation. Each role proves essential to heaven's overall campaign.

Recap: Preparing for Breakthrough

You've discovered the pattern of divine breakthrough, where long periods of underground work suddenly culminate in visible transformation. This understanding helps you maintain hope and momentum during those frustrating seasons when nothing seems to be changing despite your faithful efforts. You now recognize that lack of visible results doesn't mean lack of progress - it simply reflects the normal pattern where invisible work precedes visible change.

You've learned to recognize signs that signal approaching breakthrough. Increased resistance often indicates that systems sense they're losing control. Unusual unity among kingdom agents shows heaven positioning diverse pieces for coordinated impact. Prophetic dreams and visions provide advance notice of what's coming. Strategic relationships forming across previous boundaries create pathways for transformation to flow. These indicators help you prepare practically and spiritually for the acceleration that comes with breakthroughs.

You've explored the critical principles for stewarding breakthrough once it arrives. Protecting fragile transformation from premature publicity preserves its integrity. Resisting the urge to institutionalize too quickly maintains the flexibility essential for continued growth. Maintaining the conditions that produced breakthroughs ensures sustainable transformation rather than temporary change. Recognizing and resisting counter-movements prevents dilution, division, or distraction from undermining what heaven has established.

You've seen the bigger picture of heaven's strategy, which moves from initial infiltration through visible breakthrough to complete cultural occupation. This progression rarely happens smoothly or completely in our lifetime, but understanding it helps you recognize your specific assignment within the larger divine campaign.

So how do you apply these insights to your current situation? Start by honestly assessing where you are in the breakthrough pattern. Are you in the underground phase where little visible change appears despite faithful effort? Are you noticing the early indicators that signal approaching breakthrough? Are you experiencing the dramatic transformation of a breakthrough moment? Or are you working to establish long-term occupation in territory where breakthrough has already occurred?

If you're in the underground phase, adjust your expectations to align with heaven's breakthrough pattern. Rather than becoming discouraged by lack of visible results, recognize this as normal and necessary preparation for future transformation. Maintain faithful presence and consistent action even when nothing seems to be changing. Document even the smallest signs of movement to encourage yourself during long waiting periods.

If you're noticing signs of approaching breakthrough, begin preparing practically for the acceleration that's coming. Document the early indicators you're observing - the increased resistance, unusual unity, prophetic experiences, and strategic relationships forming. These records will provide valuable confirmation when breakthrough arrives and help others understand the process that produced it.

Prepare specific strategies for stewarding transformation when it comes. Decide in advance how you'll protect breakthrough from premature publicity without stifling appropriate celebration. Consider what minimal structures might be necessary without over-institutionalizing the movement. Identify which foundational practices must continue regardless of how busy implementation becomes.

If you're currently experiencing a breakthrough, focus on wise stewardship that preserves the integrity of what heaven has initiated. Resist pressure to expose the transformation prematurely to outside attention. Maintain the spiritual and relational foundations that created space for divine activity. Watch for counter-movements that would dilute, divide, or distract from the core transformation. Remember that breakthrough isn't the final destination but a milestone in the longer journey toward complete occupation.

If you're working in territory where breakthrough has already occurred, shift focus from producing transformation to establishing divine patterns as the new normal. Train rather than convince, helping others participate in what's already visibly successful. Work to align systems and structures with the values that drove the breakthrough. Invest particularly in the next generation who will advance occupation not through conscious effort but by living naturally from what they've always known.

Throughout all these phases, maintain the balance between celebrating progress and pursuing complete transformation. Acknowledge genuine breakthrough with appropriate gratitude while recognizing how much territory remains under opposing influence. Neither minimize what heaven has accomplished nor pretend it's more complete than reality demonstrates.

Finally, identify the next territory for infiltration even as you steward the current breakthrough. Heaven's strategy always works on multiple fronts simultaneously. While establishing occupation in areas where breakthrough has occurred, it simultaneously begins underground work in new territories. Your assignment likely includes both stewarding what's already transformed and initiating infiltration where heaven's culture remains largely absent.

The tipping point when heaven's culture breaks through provides some of the most exhilarating moments in spiritual experience. After long seasons of faithful effort with minimal visible results, seeing dramatic transformation unfold brings profound validation and joy. These breakthrough moments remind us that our labor hasn't been wasted and that divine power remains actively engaged in transforming earth.

Yet these dramatic moments represent midpoints, not endpoints, in heaven's strategy. They validate the underground work that preceded them while initiating the occupation process that must follow. Their greatest value comes not from the temporary excitement they generate but from the long-term transformation they make possible when properly stewarded.

As you align yourself with heaven's breakthrough pattern, you become an increasingly effective agent in the divine campaign that is secretly transforming earth. You develop patience for underground seasons, discernment for approaching breakthroughs, wisdom for stewarding transformation, and vision for complete occupation. Most importantly, you find your specific assignment within the larger strategy that has been advancing since time began and will continue until heaven's culture fully occupies every territory currently under opposing control.
Conclusion

The Invisible Revolution

Right now, as you read these words, heaven's culture is spreading through your neighborhood, your workplace, your city. It moves quietly, often unnoticed by those not paying attention. No news cameras capture its advance. No headlines announce its victories. Yet this invisible revolution is more real and more powerful than any political movement or social change you'll ever witness.

Throughout this journey, you've discovered something extraordinary - the culture of heaven isn't just coming someday in the distant future. It's actively infiltrating earth right now through ordinary people who respond to divine promptings. That stranger who showed you unexpected kindness when you needed it most? That conversation that shifted your perspective at exactly the right moment? That solution that appeared when all options seemed exhausted? These weren't random coincidences. They were evidence of a coordinated divine campaign that's been unfolding since the beginning of time.

This revelation changes everything about how you see the world around you. What once looked like scattered, disconnected events now reveals itself as a deliberate pattern. The person who forgave when revenge seemed justified. The business that prioritized people over profits when everyone said it would fail. The family that opened their home to strangers when others built higher fences. The artist whose work bypassed intellectual defenses and spoke directly to hearts. These weren't isolated anomalies - they were strategic insertions of heaven's reality into earth's broken systems.

You now understand that heaven's infiltration strategy deliberately works through hiddenness. Like seeds growing underground before breaking through the soil, the most important spiritual work happens beneath the surface where few notice it. This hiddenness isn't a mistake or a temporary approach - it's a deliberate divine strategy that protects transformative movements during their vulnerable early stages.

The ordinary vessel approach makes perfect sense now too. Heaven consistently chooses unlikely people to carry its most important assignments. Not because qualified people don't exist, but because limitations create space for divine power to become visible in ways that obvious strengths never could. Your perceived disqualifications - your past mistakes, your lack of training, your ongoing struggles - may actually be your greatest qualifications for the role heaven has designed specifically for you.

Your Infiltration Assignment

Now that you recognize the patterns of kingdom infiltration, it's time to fully embrace your role as a divine agent. This isn't about joining a new organization or taking on another religious obligation. It's about seeing your existing relationships, work, and daily activities as strategic opportunities for heaven's culture to flow through you into the world around you.

Your specific assignment is as unique as your fingerprints. No one else has exactly your combination of personality, experiences, relationships, and positioning. The places where you already have access - your workplace, neighborhood, family, social circles - these are your primary infiltration territories. The very limitations that once seemed to disqualify you are actually perfect qualifications for carrying heaven's culture into places that desperately need transformation.

Think about where you already have influence. The parent who shapes a family culture. The employee whose attitude affects an entire workplace. The neighbor whose presence changes the feel of a community. The artist whose creations shift how people see reality. The business owner whose values determine how resources flow. These ordinary roles become extraordinary opportunities when you recognize them as divine assignments rather than just human responsibilities.

You don't need to quit your job and become a professional religious worker to fulfill your infiltration assignment. In fact, such a move might actually take you away from the very territory heaven has positioned you to influence. The cashier who brings genuine joy to each customer interaction may be accomplishing more kingdom infiltration than the preacher addressing thousands but changing few.

The divine coincidence chains you've experienced weren't random. Those "chance" meetings that led to unexpected opportunities. Those books that fell open to exactly the page you needed to read. Those ideas that came to you in the middle of the night and wouldn't let you go. These were heaven's guidance system, positioning you precisely where you need to be for maximum impact in the divine campaign.

Your prophetic disruptions matter more than you realize. Those simple questions that made someone stop and reconsider their direction.

Those gentle observations that highlighted what others had missed. Those unexpected words that came out of your mouth and surprised even you. These moments created tiny cracks in hardened thinking where new possibilities could enter.

Your stealth compassion has been part of the strategy all along. The anonymous gifts you gave when you saw someone in need. The prayers you offered without telling the person you were praying. The kind acts you performed with no possibility of recognition or reward. These created experiences of divine love that bypassed intellectual defenses and touched hearts directly.

Your joyful presence in difficult environments hasn't been wasted. The peace you've maintained in chaotic workplaces. The genuine joy you've expressed in communities dominated by complaint and criticism. The hope you've carried into situations where despair seemed the only rational response. This presence has been shifting atmospheric conditions in ways you may never fully recognize until heaven's records are opened.

The Infiltrator's Path Forward

As you step more fully into your role as a kingdom infiltrator, several practical pathways open before you. These aren't complicated spiritual techniques requiring special training. They're simple approaches anyone can implement to become a more effective carrier of heaven's culture.

First, develop your spiritual discernment between human goodness and genuine divine activity. This distinction matters more than most people realize. Human goodness creates temporary improvements that require constant maintenance. Divine activity produces lasting transformation that continues developing long after the initial intervention. Human goodness addresses symptoms while divine activity heals root causes. As you sharpen this discernment, you'll stop wasting energy on impressive-looking religious activities that lack divine life and start investing more fully in the genuine movements of heaven's culture.

Start by paying attention to the aftertaste of different experiences. Human goodness, including religious performance, often leaves a subtle residue of pride, exhaustion, or emptiness once the initial satisfaction fades. Divine activity leaves a distinctly different aftertaste - a lingering sense of wonder, deep peace, and renewed energy that actually increases rather than decreases with time. These contrasting effects reveal the true source behind seemingly similar actions.

Second, identify which of the five invasion tactics resonates most naturally with your design. Are you particularly attuned to divine coincidence chains, noticing connections between seemingly random events? Do you have a gift for prophetic disruption, offering perspectives that create openings in rigid thinking? Does stealth compassion flow easily through you, meeting needs in ways that bypass defenses? Do you naturally carry joyful presence into difficult environments, shifting atmospheres without saying a word? Or does value-system infiltration match your approach, demonstrating better alternatives that make old patterns obsolete?

While you may operate in all these tactics at different times, one or two probably feel most natural to your personality and gifting. Focusing on these areas of natural strength creates maximum impact with minimum strain. You're not trying to become someone else but rather embracing how heaven has specifically designed you as an infiltration agent.

Third, create or join a small community that embodies the four components of heaven's culture. Faith in the divine that transforms how you see everything else. Heavenly priorities that redefine success according to love expressed rather than resources accumulated. Divine revelation that provides guidance beyond human wisdom. Kingdom norms that establish patterns of forgiveness, generosity, truthful speech, and joy even in suffering.

These cultural components thrive best in community rather than isolation. Even two or three people committed to embodying heaven's alternative culture create a powerful incubator where divine patterns can take root and strengthen. This doesn't require starting a new organization or program. It might be a weekly meal with friends, a regular coffee meeting with colleagues, or a neighborhood gathering in your home. The form matters less than the consistent practice of heaven's culture within relationships.

Fourth, learn to recognize and address cultural systems rather than just individual symptoms. Most problems that seem personal actually reflect systemic issues operating beneath the surface. The employee struggling with motivation works within a company culture that quenches initiative. The teenager making destructive choices lives in a family system that makes healthy options difficult to sustain. The neighbor who keeps to themselves exists in a community where isolation has become normal.

As you develop system-level perception, you'll stop wasting energy treating symptoms and start addressing root causes. You'll identify the unwritten rules and shared assumptions that lock people into harmful patterns. You'll find the leverage points where small changes can trigger cascading effects throughout larger systems. This approach multiplies your impact far beyond what individual-focused efforts could ever achieve.

Fifth, prepare yourself for the resistance that inevitably comes when heaven's culture successfully infiltrates established systems. This opposition isn't a sign that something's wrong with your approach. It's evidence that your presence is making a real difference. Systems don't waste resources fighting what poses no threat to their control.

Develop supernatural resilience through perspective shifts that transform how you interpret resistance. Establish rhythms of strategic rest that prepare you for sustained effectiveness. Build connections with others who understand the infiltration process and can provide encouragement during difficult seasons. Learn to celebrate opposition as confirmation you're on the right track rather than evidence you've somehow failed.

Finally, position yourself to recognize and steward breakthrough moments when they arrive. After long periods of underground work with little visible result, heaven's culture eventually reaches tipping points where transformation suddenly becomes visible. These moments require careful stewardship to protect fragile breakthroughs from premature exposure, resist the urge to institutionalize too quickly, and maintain the conditions that produced the transformation in the first place.

Pay attention to the signs that signal approaching breakthrough - increased resistance, unusual unity among kingdom agents, prophetic dreams and visions pointing to the same outcomes, and strategic relationships forming across previous boundaries. These indicators help you prepare practically and spiritually for the acceleration that comes when underground work suddenly produces visible transformation.

As you walk this infiltrator's path, remember that you're not alone. All around the world, ordinary people just like you are responding to the same divine strategy. The quiet mother whose prayers are reshaping a school system. The ethical business leader whose decisions are transforming an industry. The faithful friend whose consistent love is healing generational wounds. The creative artist whose work is bypassing intellectual barriers and touching hearts directly. Together, you form an invisible network more powerful than any human organization could ever be.

What once looked random in your life now reveals itself as strategic divine positioning. That unexpected job change that made no sense at the time. The relationship that connected you with people outside your normal circles. The interest that drew you to develop unusual skills. The struggle that gave you compassion you couldn't have gained any other way. These weren't detours or accidents - they were preparation for your specific role in heaven's infiltration strategy.

The culture of heaven is already transforming earth through ordinary people who have recognized and responded to divine promptings. Some know exactly what they're doing. Others have no idea they're being used as agents of heaven's culture - they're simply following the love, joy, peace, and wisdom flowing through them into a broken world. Either way, the revolution advances, one coincidence chain, one disruptive word, one compassionate act, one atmosphere shift, and one transformed value system at a time.

You now stand at a crossroads. You can continue seeing the events around you as random coincidences and isolated problems requiring human solutions. Or you can recognize the coordinated divine campaign operating right beneath the surface of everyday reality. You can maintain the comfortable illusion that what happens in your ordinary life doesn't really matter in the grand scheme of things. Or you can embrace your strategic assignment as a carrier of heaven's culture into the specific territories where you've been positioned.

The choice is yours. But know this - heaven's infiltration will continue with or without your conscious participation. The question isn't whether divine culture will eventually transform earth. The question is whether you'll experience the profound joy and purpose that comes from recognizing and embracing your role in this cosmic revolution that's been unfolding since the beginning of time and will continue until heaven's culture fully occupies every territory currently under opposing control.

The invasion has already begun. Heaven's culture is breaking through. And you are invited to be part of the most important movement in human history - not as a distant observer but as an active agent carrying divine reality into the very places that need it most. Your ordinary life is the perfect disguise for this extraordinary assignment. The infiltration starts now.

The Invitation

I hope this message finds you well. I wanted to share something truly special with you – an invitation to experience the Kingdom of God. This might be a new concept for you, but it's a journey that can bring profound peace, joy, and purpose to your life.

The idea of being "born again" might sound a bit mysterious, but it's essentially about experiencing a spiritual rebirth. It's about opening your heart and mind to a new way of living, one that is guided by love, compassion, and a deep connection with God. When we talk about being born again, we mean allowing God's Spirit to transform us from within, giving us a fresh start and a new perspective on life.

Jesus once said, "Unless someone is born again, from above, they cannot see the Kingdom of God." This means that to truly understand and experience the fullness of God's love and the beauty of His Kingdom, we need to undergo this spiritual transformation. It's like seeing the world with new eyes, where everything is filled with hope and possibility.

I invite you to explore this journey of being born again. It's a personal and profound experience that can lead to a deeper understanding of yourself and your purpose in life. If you have any questions or would like to know more, I'm here to help and support you.

To be born again and receive Christ as your Savior and King is a deeply personal and transformative experience. Here are some steps to guide you through this spiritual journey:

1. **Acknowledge Your Need for Christ:** Recognize that you need a Savior. This means understanding that we all fall short and need God's grace and forgiveness.

2. **Believe in Jesus Christ:** Have faith that Jesus Christ is the Son of God, who died for our sins and rose again. This belief is the foundation of being born again.

3. **Confess Your Sins:** Open your heart to God and confess your sins. This is an important step in seeking forgiveness and starting anew.

4. **Invite Christ into Your Life:** Pray and ask Jesus to come into your heart and life. You can say something like, "Lord Jesus, I believe you are the Son of God. I confess my sins and ask for your forgiveness. Please come into my heart and be my Savior and King. Transform me and guide me in your ways."

5. **Commit to Following Christ:** Make a commitment to follow Jesus and live according to His teachings. This involves reading the Bible, praying, and seeking fellowship with other believers.

6. **Experience the Transformation:** As you invite Christ into your life, you will begin to experience a spiritual rebirth. This transformation will bring new perspectives, peace, and purpose to your life.

Remember, this journey is unique to each person, and it's okay to have questions and seek guidance along the way. If you need support or have any questions, feel free to reach out.

Terry Kashian - **altarlife@gmail.com**

www.ingramcontent.com/pod-product-compliance
Lightning Source LLC
Chambersburg PA
CBHW052118030426
42335CB00025B/3036